HAYNES GREAT CARS

MORGAN
PLUS 8

HAYNES GREAT CARS

MORGAN
PLUS 8

MICHAEL SCARLETT

First published in February 2009

A catalogue record for this book is available from the British Library

ISBN 978 1 84425 354 8

Library of Congress catalog card number 2008926355

Published by Haynes Publishing, Sparkford,
Yeovil, Somerset BA22 7JJ, England
Tel: 01963 442030 Fax: 01963 440001
Int. tel: +44 1963 442030 Int. fax: +44 1963 440001
E-mail: sales@haynes.co.uk
Web site: www.haynes.co.uk

Haynes North America Inc.
861 Lawrence Drive, Newbury Park, California 91320, USA

Designed by James Robertson

Printed and bound in Great Britain by J. H. Haynes & Co. Ltd

Contents

INTRODUCTION

My first encounter with the Morgan Plus 8 in the shape of MMC 11, which I learnt much later was the second prototype, was as a Road Tester (writer of car tests) on *Autocar* magazine. It turned out to be the very first full Road Test conducted by any motoring publication (published in the 12 September 1968 issue), accompanying the first full description of the car, illustrated with an *Autocar* cutaway drawing by Vic Berris.

Fellow *Autocar* Road Tester David Thomas and I took MMC 11 to the Motor Industry Research Association (MIRA) proving grounds in the Midlands to measure acceleration, braking, steady-speed fuel consumption, and lesser data. By the standards of the time, this Plus 8 was very accelerative, recording 0–60mph in 6.7sec, 0–100 in 18.4sec, and running on to 120mph in 42.9sec. These figures reflected the car's wonderfully low kerb weight of 1,979lb, the claimed power and peak torque of its ex-Oldsmobile Rover V8 3.5-litre engine (160.5bhp at 5,200rpm and 210lb ft at 3,000rpm), and (as far as acceleration from 60 to 120mph went) its relatively high aerodynamic drag figure.

The only weakness of this re-creation of a post-Vintage sports car noticed on that day occurred during the testing of maximum braking, when the car was shaken by a curious vibration. This turned out to be a highly visible twisting of the transverse tubular ladder-like frame across the front of the car, whose ends carried the famous Morgan sliding-pillar

independent front suspension. We felt this arose because that first Plus 8 borrowed much of its chassis from the much lower-powered, lesser-tyred Morgan Plus 4, the larger rolling gear somewhat overloading the chassis during peak braking.

Next, we took the car to Belgium, to measure its two-way average maximum speed on the Jabbeke autoroute straight, made famous earlier by the maximum speed demonstrations of, first, the Jaguar XK120, and later the first Triumph TR2. The only downside to this road, which then had no speed limit, was that it had aged somewhat by the late 1960s. This was shown by the way the road either side of any bridges had subsided a little compared

Right: Second prototype of 1968 Plus 8 as Road Tested by Autocar.

Above: A 1989 Plus 8 in all its glory.

to each bridge, due presumably to the better foundations of the bridge relative to the approach road. This produced a perhaps half-inch ridge bump across the road where it gave way to the bridge – not a serious problem for a fast saloon of the time.

Having checked out the stretch of autoroute as suitable for 'maxing' – straight and level, with no exits or entries or other obvious hazards – we then re-attached the Road Test fifth wheel electric speedometer, got out our stopwatch, and set off, right foot flat to the floor. The speed rose encouragingly until the fifth wheel showed we had achieved the maximum in that direction – 125mph (it recorded 123 the other way, for a mean maximum of 124mph).

The car was now close to the selected measured kilometre, preceded by a bridge. We got to the beginning of the bridge and were somewhat surprised by what then happened – there was a noticeable, if not too loud, bang as the car jumped on hitting the joint between road and bridge. However, it was enough for the engine

speed to rise momentarily as the back wheels came off the surface; we had flown briefly but definitely.

Overall, we loved that first Plus 8, even

if it did suggest that some development was due – read on to learn more about the work that went into making the Morgan Plus 8 the success it was in its 37-year life.

Acknowledgements

My first thanks must go to Charles Morgan, for finding the time in his busy life as managing director of the Morgan Motor Co to grant me a valuable interview and provide a huge amount of historical information. Equally valued were interviews with racing engineer Chris Lawrence (who won fame as the very successful driver of his Lawrencetune Morgan Plus 4 at Le Mans), Mark Aston (who after time in the sales department, was Morgan's technical director, then assistant managing director during most of the Plus 8's production life), and Professor Jim Randle with Keith Helfet, for explaining their involvement with the beginnings of the Aero 8.

Thanks are due also to those Morgan owners who kindly allowed their cars to be used for the specially commissioned studio photographs by John Colley and Tom Wood. The owners are: Bob Cragg (1969 BRG Plus 8), John Carver (1977 cream/brown Plus 8), Chris Balch (1989 red Plus 8 injection), Peter and Loretta Simpson (1999 silver Plus 8 4.6-litre), and Colin Trott (2007 silver/blue Aero 8 Series 3).

Closer to home, I owe a huge debt of gratitude for his patience and understanding to Steve Rendle, commissioning editor of the Specialist Book Publishing Division of Haynes Publishing. Finally, I am grateful to my family for putting up with the unsocial aspects of a husband and father buried in the work of researching and writing.

Michael Scarlett, February 2009

Left: *View of cockpit on second prototype Plus 8.*

Above: The **Autocar** *Road Tests Plus 8 at rest beside the Jabbeke autoroute with the ridge-making bridge in the background.*

Below: **Autocar** *Road Tester David Thomas attaches the fifth wheel prior to the Jabbeke maximum speed runs in July 1968.*

DESIGN AND DEVELOPMENT

Founded in 1909 by H. F. S. Morgan, the son of a parson, the Morgan Motor Company has remained in the ownership of the Morgan family ever since. H. F. S.'s grandson, Charles Morgan, is managing director of the company today. For much of its first 100 years, it exclusively produced three-wheelers – not in any way like most of the handful of three-wheeled economy cars conceived since the Second World War – with a basic design that made the best of the fundamental problem of three-wheeled cars, their inherent handicap in terms of anti-roll-over stability. Morgan three-wheelers did this by laying the car out with the base of the triangle formed by the three wheels at the front, and installing the engine – the heaviest concentration of mass in such a car – between the wheels, which pulled the centre of gravity forward to increase the turning moment needed for the car to roll over in a bend.

Right: The second prototype Plus 8.

Although there was an experimental four-wheeler made in 1914, prompted by exclusion of Morgan's three-wheelers from some events, and a family four-seater put into production in the following year, Morgan first properly ventured into four-wheeled sports cars in December 1935, leading ultimately from a base of 1½- to 2-litre cars to the subject of this book, the Morgan Plus 8, which appeared publicly in August 1968. The Morgan four-wheeler design and engineering remained faithful to much of the original concept. A traditional frame type of chassis, using Z-section steel longerons, was joined crosswise by top-hat section members, except at the front end, where a transverse tubular frame ran across the chassis. The ends were formed by pillars on which were mounted stub axles, forged with inward extensions top and bottom, each pierced vertically to slide up and down on the pillars and sprung by concentric coil springs.

Thus was formed the long-established Morgan sliding pillar independent front suspension, which the company had used since its foundation; the system had been patented by H. F. S. Morgan back in 1910. At the rear, there was a live axle, located and sprung by five-leaf semi-elliptic springs (six leaves became an option later). Damping was provided by Armstrong units, telescopic in front, and lever-arm type at the back. Steering relied on a worm and nut steering box. The body was built on traditional prewar coachbuilding principles, fully detachable from the chassis, and using steel panels on an ash frame, whose slight flexibility happily accommodated the low torsional rigidity of the chassis.

The Rover V8 engine

From 1965, the late Peter Morgan, son of H. F. S. Morgan, was looking for more power for the most powerful Morgan Plus 4, which until then had latterly been dependent on the ex-Triumph 2000 2.1-litre four-cylinder engine. His search was sharpened by the fact that Triumph was changing this engine for a 2.5-litre six-cylinder unit, which was too long and high for the Plus 4. Other possibilities included the Lotus Twin Cam unit (discounted on reliability grounds) and the Ford V6 – like the new Triumph engine, too large and too heavy.

In May of the following year, Peter Wilks (a Rover director in charge of design and engineering and an old school friend of Peter Morgan's) approached Morgan to see if it would consider a Rover takeover. In the course of the meeting, Wilks mentioned the adoption by his company of the 3½-litre aluminium-alloy Buick-Oldsmobile V8. This prompted Peter Morgan to ask if it could be made available to Morgan. Wilks replied that yes, such a possibility was feasible.

So where did this engine come from historically, and what prompted General

Motors to design and build it? Briefly, there was a fashion in the US car market for a relatively short time for so-called compact cars, smaller than the traditional Detroit giants. What GM knew as the X100 215cu in (3,582cc) 3.5in x 2.8in (88.9 x 71.12mm) 'over-square' lightweight V8 engine was designed for such cars. The X100 was in fact produced in considerable numbers for Buick's Special, Pontiac's Tempest, and in a slightly more powerful version for the Oldsmobile Cutlass F85, up to the point where the decline in the compact car fashion caused GM to stop making it. In its Buick/Pontiac normal version, with a twin choke Rochester carburettor, an 8.8:1 compression ratio, and a maximum engine speed of 5,300rpm, it produced 155bhp at 4,600rpm and 220lb ft of torque at 2,400rpm.

Peter Wilks successfully negotiated the purchase of the engine design, engine production equipment, and a number of the engines. He also acquired the services and invaluable knowledge of former Buick engine designer and chief engineer Joe Turley, who came to England near the end of his time at Buick to work with the Rover engine designers on modifying its design for use first of all in the Rover P5, the Rover company having got a licence to manufacture the engine in January 1965. The Rover team worked on the design for several years up to its appearance in the P5 in 1967.

The changes included abandoning the original high-silicon aluminium-alloy die-castings for the cylinder block and head in favour of traditional sand-casting, which allowed slightly thicker cylinder walls. The cylinder block was unusual in American V8 design in having its crankcase walls extended below the crankshaft centreline by a modest amount (approximately equivalent to the depth of the main bearing caps), a feature inherited from the V8 for an earlier (1951) XP300 experimental car, and this classic strengthening feature was carried over into the Rover version. A number of other design features continued, such as the hydraulic self-adjusting tappets and a crankshaft whose four crankpins each carried two connecting rod big-ends, one from each side. Cylinder liners remained centrifugally-cast iron, but instead of being cast in place during the making of the block, were pressed in place; they were thick enough to provide a maximum of 0.020in of reboring capability.

Other modifications included better breathing for the engine provided by the new inlet manifold to allow the replacement of the Rochester carburettor with two SU HS6s with 1in diameter

Below: The Rover 3.5-litre V8 engine as installed in the Rover 3500 in April 1968 and subsequently used by Morgan, which replaced the Borg-Warner automatic gearbox shown with a manual Moss one and rearranged some ancillaries.

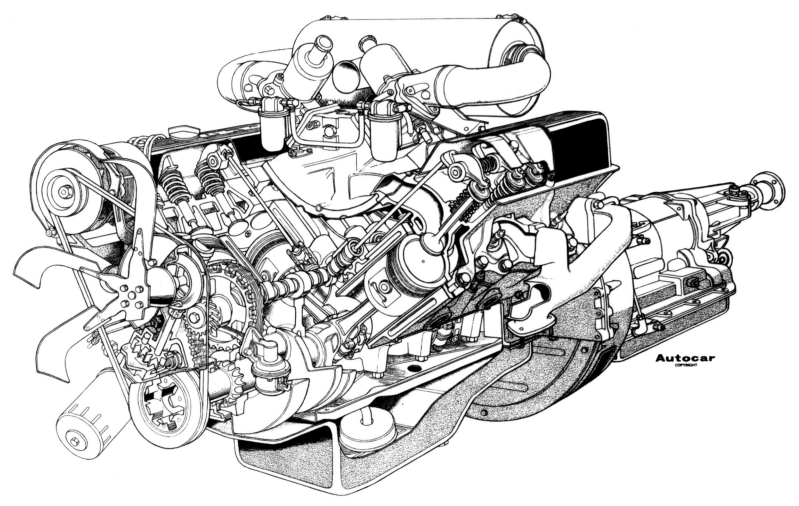

Autocar
COPYRIGHT

choke tubes and the usual SU manual mixture enrichment control as opposed to 'choking-off' the air in place of the previous automatic choke. Each SU was mounted largely horizontally, if with roughly 15° of downdraught inclination. Compression ratio was increased considerably, to 10.5:1, demanding the use of 100-octane petrol. Power output was increased to 168bhp at 5,200rpm and torque became 210lb ft at 2,700rpm. Ignition and electrics were changed from the previous AC-Delco system to a Lucas 35D8 distributor, Champion L87 sparking plugs, a Lucas 11AC 45-amp alternator, and a pre-engaged Lucas M45G starter motor.

There was a new design of cooling fan, with considerably bent-over tips to its five blades; these were closely analogous to the vertical fin extensions to the wing tips nowadays seen on many large airliners, in that they considerably reduced the aerodynamic breakaway which otherwise occurs, thus improving lift on a plane. Straight-ended blades produce noise from turbulence, which the bent-over tips avoided in the interests of engine refinement. The cooling system itself ran at 15psi and had a capacity of 16 pints.

In Rover form – and therefore first Morgan Plus 8 models – the engine followed mostly normal good engine design practice. A chain drive was provided for the single camshaft in the vee, with a skew gear at the front of the camshaft driving the distributor and oil pump; sprockets for the chain drive were made from sintered iron for the chain wheel on the crankshaft and aluminium alloy with nylon-coated teeth for the camshaft chain wheel. The camshaft itself ran in traditional Babbitt metal bearings, backed by steel rings. The two valves per cylinder were 1.495in diameter for the inlet valves and 1.308in diameter for the exhausts, sitting in piston-ring-iron valve seats.

Crankshaft journals were 2.30in diameter for the main bearings and 0.80in long, with 2in diameter crankpins for the connecting rod big ends. Con-rod little ends carried 0.875in diameter and 2.86in long gudgeon pins, press-fitted into the little ends. Piston sealing against

combustion gas blow-by consisted of two compression rings and a single oil control ring to each piston. The sump capacity was 8.5 pints, feeding the gear-type oil pump that worked at 30–40psi through a full-flow oil filter mounted below the pump.

Thus the Plus 8 engine ended up basically to Rover SD1 3500 specification and tune – not that the Plus 8, incidentally, was the first V8-engined

Morgan, the company having toyed with the side-valve Ford V8 engine from the Ford Pilot saloon before the Second World War. The idea was dropped because of the need for much better braking on the car to cope with the greatly added performance and the tiresome fact of vehicle taxation of the time, which was based on the notorious RAC horsepower rating system, making the V8 car horribly costly to tax.

Adapting the V8 for Morgan

Returning to the Rover-sourced V8, it had the same bore and stroke of 88.9 x 71.12mm, providing a swept volume of 3,528cc, a power output of 151bhp (DIN) at 5,200rpm, and maximum torque of 210lb ft at 2,750rpm on 100-octane fuel. Its aluminium alloy feature was shared by both the cylinder block and crankcase. Cylinders had 'dry' steel liners, meaning that coolant was not directly in contact with the liners themselves. The five-bearing crankshaft was in cast iron and was fully counter-weighted with a torsional vibration damper at the front end.

Each cylinder head had cross-flow ports

running into part-spherical combustion chambers. Valve gear remained two per cylinder, worked in the usual V8 style by short pushrods from a centre camshaft via hydraulic tappets. The inlet valves were fed by two SU carburettors, using in the Morgan's case a Land-Rover inlet manifold that kept the SUs lower to more nearly suit the Plus 8 underbonnet height, though not low enough to avoid the first prototype sporting small 'power bulges' in the bonnet. (The original American Holley downdraught carburettor was too tall, for Rover's application in the first place and certainly for the Morgan's low bonnet.) The sump, of

Above: View of one bank and one SU carburettor, plus part of the opposite SU, of a Rover V8 engine in a 1969 Plus 8. Note the dent made in the top of the air cleaner, necessary on early cars to clear the bonnet hinge due to the extra height of the engine when mounted on, instead of between, the chassis side members.

Above: View of the slightly inclined pair of SU HS6 carburettors.

Right: Detail shot of dent in air cleaner to clear bonnet hinge in early cars.

daily chassis lubrication system by pedal from the cockpit) by 2in ahead of the scuttle and widening it slightly.

To assist the design work, in the initial absence of a working V8, Rover had provided a non-working mock-up of the engine, which was helpful to some extent but not for all development. Maurice therefore took a working Buick original, one of three he had obtained at the auction of Gordon-Keeble's equipment when that company sold up, the other two of which he had used, oddly enough, in a Rover 2000TC well before Rover got round to the notion, and in a Cooper hill-climb car. Rover kindly uprated its structure to match what would be in production, once it started. Most notable was the stiffening of the main bearing supports, as an addition to the extensions of the cylinder block die-casting below the crankshaft centreline to increase beam and torsional stiffness. This was accomplished by Rover recasting the blocks using the traditional sand-casting technique.

The extra width and size of the V8 did require some changes. Most obvious was how to overcome the way the engine obstructed the steering column. The answer was the adoption of a column universally jointed through its lower length that could be led round the engine, in the process endowing the Plus 8 with a modern passive safety feature. A minor detail required to allow the Rover engine under the bonnet's central hinge was a slight flattening of the air-cleaner casing. Similarly, the alternator demanded a clearance recess in the inner part of one wing.

On the engine itself, the boss on the front of the water pump, which in the Rover carried the engine-driven fan and its pulley, was machined off and a slimmer pulley fitted to suit the run of the alternator belt. The consequent replacement of the traditional engine-driven cooling fan with a Wood-Jeffreys thermostatically controlled electric fan between the radiator and front cross-frame – an unlooked-for advance in engine efficiency (removing the power lost by driving a normal fan) – was accompanied by a filler on top of a remote swirl pot, as there wasn't enough space for the usual under-bonnet cowl filler.

course, was a 'wet' one, as opposed to a dry-sump used in most competition engines. On the early Plus 8s, two downpipes from each exhaust manifold, joined by a rear-mounted balance pipe, led into a single pipe and silencer system.

Maurice Owen, a competition car engineer who had previously worked for the Laystall Formula 1 racing team, had previously offered his services to Peter Morgan should any sort of special Morgan be needed to be designed and built. Here was an ideal opportunity to take advantage of Owen's abilities – Morgan personnel were too heavily committed then to take on such a major job – so Peter Morgan invited Maurice Owen to join the Morgan company in 1966. He took Maurice to meet Rover engineers in the autumn of that year, and it was quickly established that, in most important respects, the Rover V8 was compact enough to be accommodated within the envelope dictated by the Plus 4 chassis front end. In due course it was decided to increase the space for the new power unit by lengthening the Rubery Owen-made chassis (with its traditional

Transmission

Morgan had established that its usual Moss gearbox was strong enough for the extra power and torque of the V8 when working on the relative lightness of the car. However, marrying the V8 to the gearbox and its non-synchromesh first gear was a small challenge. Maurice overcame this by welding the output end of a Morgan bellhousing to the wider end of a Buick bellhousing and machining a suitably longer (if still short) primary shaft, enclosed in a cast aluminium alloy tube. Morgan's usual direct mechanical operation of the clutch now gave way to an hydraulic slave cylinder, a driver aid of some value, given the higher clutch clamping load demanded by the larger power unit.

The marriage also required a redesigned flywheel to suit the clutch and the starter motor position had to be changed from the Rover original. The consequent position of the gearbox gave the benefit of a short gear lever sited immediately above the gearbox selectors, with no intervening linkages to add lost motion. To avoid, or at any rate minimise, axle tramp under over-enthusiastic acceleration, a limited slip differential was fitted. The final drive came from Salisbury, its 7HA type with the highest-geared ratio on offer, 3.58:1, in spite of Morgan quite rightly knowing that the car would happily take higher gearing in the 3.4:1 region – this came later.

Left: The short gear lever acted direct on the selectors.

Chassis design

The Plus 8 chassis was a good example of the structural simplicity of the typical pre-unitary construction frame for passenger cars. It was basically two Z-section steel beams running straight and parallel between the back end supporting the outer ends of the semi-elliptic leaf springs for the rear axle, and the front bulkhead

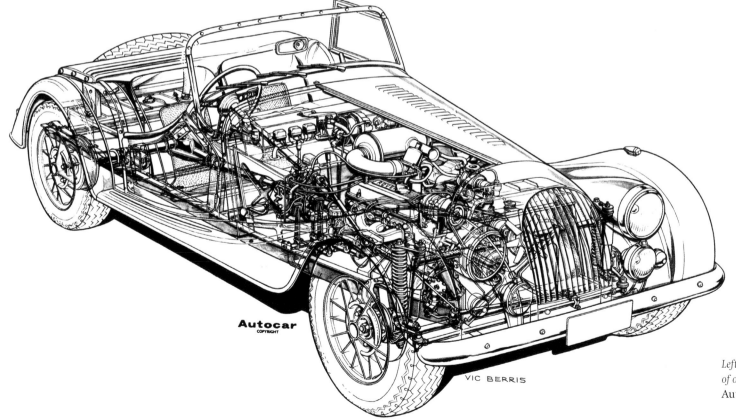

Left: Cutaway drawing of original Plus 8 by Autocar's Vic Berris.

Right: Drawing of Plus 8 chassis frame, displaying its Z-section side members and overall simplicity.

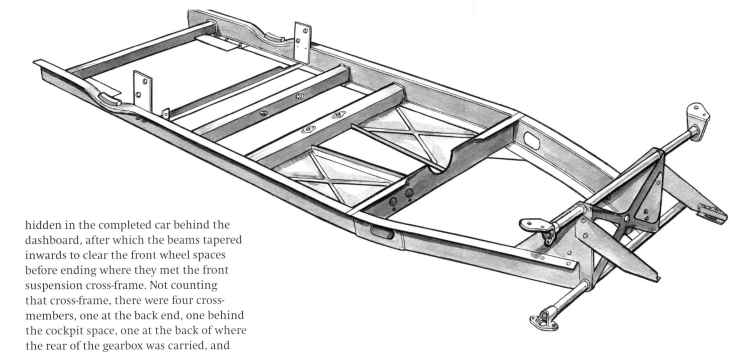

hidden in the completed car behind the dashboard, after which the beams tapered inwards to clear the front wheel spaces before ending where they met the front suspension cross-frame. Not counting that cross-frame, there were four cross-members, one at the back end, one behind the cockpit space, one at the back of where the rear of the gearbox was carried, and the fourth under the front bulkhead.

One big difference from the traditional passenger car chassis, which nearly always arched itself over the rear axle, was that the Morgan's low build encouraged the designers to set the Z-section longerons to run under the back axle, so in side view they ran straight and level. There were two cross-members from which the leaf springs at the rear worked, one at the back whose spring brackets each carried a traditional shackle, the other set behind the cockpit area carrying its spring bracket, from which the front end of each leaf spring pivoted. The leaf springs were placed just inside the

Below: Front suspension cross-frame without the sliding pillars and their springs.

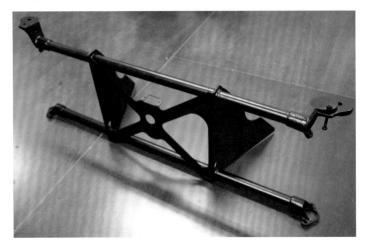

longerons, which themselves had their top surfaces curved towards the bottom before curving back up again so that the Z-sections were of shallow section at this point, to clear the axle set above the chassis. Lubrication of the sliding pillar front suspension continued with the traditional method of the driver pressing an added pedal in the cockpit to pump oil to the bearing surfaces on a daily or every 200-mile basis.

A few changes had to be made to this traditional Morgan chassis, in the shape of strengthening the join between the

longerons and the front cross-member, to cope with the increase in torque – not engine weight, as in fact the aluminium-alloy V8 was lighter than the Plus 4's 2,138cc Triumph four-cylinder engine. Mainly as a stiffening measure, the floor under the footwells was changed from wood to steel and the joins between the bulkhead cross-members were reinforced with triangular gussets. Similarly the platform carrying the new fuel tank, larger because of the higher fuel consumption of the V8, was in steel plate.

Suspension and steering

In the suspension area, some failures of the front stub axles occurred under the added loading of the extra performance and larger wheel-tyre combination, so the Plus 8 had some stronger examples. Also in the front suspension, the upper spring carrying the front end in the sliding pillar arrangement had one coil removed compared to the Plus 4, whilst the much shorter rebound lower spring was left unaltered.

The V8's extra power and torque could clearly momentarily 'wind up' the rear semi-elliptic springs to cause axle tramp, so Maurice Owen gave the springs a 7° fall from the rear by dropping the front

shackle pivot and raising the rear one. The inclination of the rear leaf springs also endowed the chassis with slight geometric understeer, aiding stability. There was a small increase in rear axle vertical movement, set at around 4½in.

Mark Aston, later a senior employee of Morgan, has contributed a number of comments on the Plus 8 to this book and is most interesting about the history of the damping methods used on the Plus 8 suspension. He threw some light on the experience I recounted earlier in this book when I was involved in the first ever magazine Road Test of what turned out

Left: Front suspension spring and the smaller rebound spring.

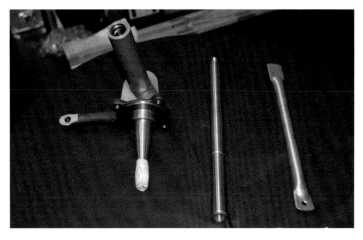

Below: Left to right: Front suspension stub axle with steering arm, sliding pillar sleeve, and triangulating brace for front cross-member.

Right: Morgan's long-established sliding pillar front suspension seen without springs but with stub axle (to carry wheel bearings) and steering arm.

to be the pre-production prototype of the Plus 8 (registration number MMC 11) and experienced a short 'flight' after hitting a ridge bump on the Belgian autoroute *Autocar* used for measuring the car's maximum speed.

'You could get that on a lip sort of bump like that because, on the early cars, the front suspension was stiffer than the back and dampers were very stiff – that was one of the first things I changed with the car when I got involved, I softened the dampers off. I softened the dampers off from the original settings, because people used to put Konis on and they said "Oh we've stiffened the

front suspension up, so it's much better than the standard one," which was hokum – Konis are about 25 per cent softer, which was what was making the difference.

'It's a conversation I had with Peter, because the Armstrong shock absorbers they were using they had used from way back – the Plus 8 had lever-arm dampers on the back and the tendency when you hit a lip bump like that was that the back would sit because there was very little bump resistance, but the rebound resistance on those Armstrong lever arms was very strong, therefore, of course, all that effectively happened was that the

returning force was too weak, so that the axle didn't go anywhere, it just stopped, which was why you took off.'

In a passive safety move that was early for any British car of the time, Morgan selected an AC-Delco-Saginaw mesh-tubed column that, if compressed in a serious frontal collision, would collapse telescopically rather than pushing the column and steering wheel into the driver, a requirement then still under discussion for future American safety law. The Cam Gears worm and nut steering box gave the car 3½ turns lock to lock; the steering wheel was a 15in Astrali.

Below left: Rear suspension five-leaf spring and securing U-bolts.

Below: Rear axle Armstrong lever damper and link.

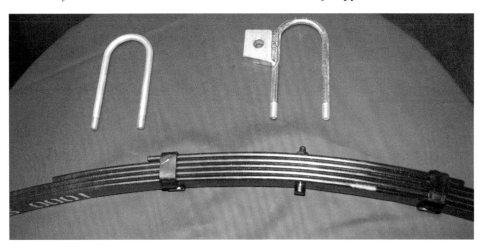

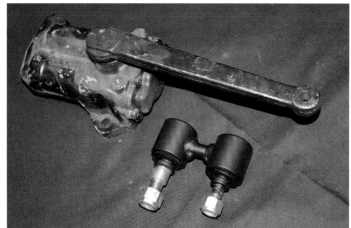

Wheels and brakes

Below: The 15in magnesium alloy wheels had a five-nut fixing.

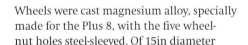

Wheels were cast magnesium alloy, specially made for the Plus 8, with the five wheel-nut holes steel-sleeved. Of 15in diameter with 5.5in wide rims, they were shod with Dunlop SP Sport Aquajet 185-15 tyres. At this time, the wire wheels traditionally expected on and associated with sports cars were found wanting in strength in a car of the Plus 8's performance, hence the fitting of cast magnesium-alloy wheels with the five wheel nut holes steel-sleeved as standard for the car.

Mark Aston is also interesting about the tyres used on the Plus 8: 'The other thing you used to get a lot were the tyres in those days – the tyre quality was not startling. The original Dunlop Aquajet SP Sport, which was a Jaguar tyre, which (compared with most tyres of the time) was very good in the wet.

'But there was a lot of tread depth on it to accommodate the Aquajet system and they'd made the tread relatively hard, so you had a very hard tyre, and the last thing you really want on a Morgan is a hard tyre, because the suspension wasn't that mobile.

The problem was really the damping – Maurice had gone for a fairly stiff damper set-up on the front, relatively little bump but relatively stiff resistance, and we later changed it. The management wanted gas dampers later on, which actually made it worse, making the ride more bobbly – the car was better off with something like the Koni, which is a normal hydraulic damper, because you had relatively little suspension travel and the suspension, particularly the front suspension, needs to get moving, so you needed to hit it with a reasonable bump.

'In the early days, we used to get a lot of problems with the tyres being very hard and then later on they switched to the Dunlop SP57 on the 14-inch Millrace wheel, which were not an improvement. They were oversize and poorly designed, because they had very big, softish sidewalls, so that when owners who used to put their cars away for a reasonable

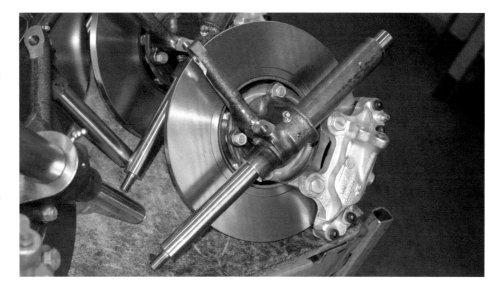

Left: Front brakes used 11in solid discs.

period of time, for example in the winter, took the car out again when the sun came out, they'd go for a nice drive in the countryside.

'And what they ended up with were flats which developed in the tyres, not because they'd been ground off in over-braking, but simply because they had been sitting for some time – and the flats wouldn't come out, because it was fairly funny rubber. So, of course, what happened then was that when those flats were out of sequence after you've gone over a bump, the car rode most oddly, so that we used to get people coming in and saying, "The suspension's all gone," and stuff like that, to which we'd reply, "It'll be the tyres." Many of them did not believe us, but if the car was then brought in and put on a set of something like Michelin XWX, a much better tyre, they'd go off up the road and come back and say, "Oh, it's completely cured."

'We had a particularly good bit in Malvern, where you turned from the factory and went down a side road, and there was a bump in the road like your one that you came across during that road test of MMC 11 and a couple of steps after in the road. Go over this and, if you had one of these cars with tyres like that, you could guarantee even at 35–40mph it would misbehave – swap the tyres over and it was fine.

'So the Plus 8's ride bothers were down to tyres a little bit as well. One of the things that was done was they used to put these Koni dampers on at a forward-facing angle to make a frame over the top; Koni developed it with somebody – and that used to make the back a lot more controllable; they used to put the Konis on the front too which worked pretty well.'

The brakes, later made dual-circuit, depended on Girling 11in diameter discs in front with larger '14P' calipers (the Plus 4 depended on smaller '12P' calipers), whilst at the back, the drums were standard Plus 4 size, 9in by 1in wide. The handbrake was a traditional sports car fly-off type. (This is released simply by briefly pulling the handbrake on a little, instead of the usual hand-released pawl, with its attendant clicking if the handbrake is applied without pressing the button in the handle briefly to release the pawl.)

Body

Inside the cockpit, Maurice Owen designed and built prototype bucket seats, which he took to Restall as a pattern for its production of seats for Morgan thereafter. The fitting of separate, adjustable bucket seats was a novelty for Morgan, which had traditionally used a bench seat. In the cockpit, the dashboard was now covered with Ambla (leathercloth) and what occupant heating was provided was via a recirculating unit. Its switches were the flush rocker type in the interests of passenger safety. The overall layout was not ideal for the car's drivers; the speedometer

Below: Separate bucket seats, a facia covered in Ambla, and flush rocker switches were features of the first Plus 8s.

Right: The Plus 8 retained traditional sidescreens, though many other sports cars by then had winding windows.

Below: The second prototype Plus 8 photographed by the author in 1968.

placed in front of the passenger being difficult to see and the rev counter in the traditional sports car position on the driver's side somewhat obscured by the steering wheel. Side windows remained Perspex. The 12-volt battery lived under the cockpit floor.

The body of the prototype was basically identical to a Plus 4 body, except for the bonnet. Because the chassis was basically the slightly narrower Plus 4 one, the engine had to be mounted on top of the chassis, instead of between it as in later production cars, so its greater height meant that the

bonnet had to accommodate the tops of the carburettors with two small bulges. This was the obvious visible major respect in which OUY 200E, as the prototype was registered, differed from the second prototype MMC 11 (the car mentioned in the Introduction) and all subsequent production Plus 8s. Being based on a Plus 4, it was also of course 2in shorter, ending up with major dimensions of an 8ft 2in wheelbase, tracks of 4ft 1in front and 4ft 3in rear, and overall dimensions of 12ft 8in length, 4ft 9in width, and a height with the hood up of 4ft 2in.

Developing the Plus 8

It was mid February of 1967 when, after a small delay due to an alternator problem, OUY 200E first ran, soon after midnight on the crucial day. Both Maurice Owen and, next morning, Peter Morgan were delighted and even surprised at how the car drove and performed, so that matters looked all set for production. However, the motoring fates intruded, for in the previous month Leyland had taken over the Rover company. The frustration was that Rover was no longer in a position to authorise supply to Morgan immediately – a pain for Peter Morgan, who had had plans to launch the car at the March 1967 Geneva Show.

The first sign of a reaction from the new group was an invitation from Harry Webster, boss of Standard-Triumph, to Peter Morgan to have lunch with him. In the event, lunch was followed by a tour of the Triumph engine manufacturing plant, where the Triumph Stag's 3-litre V8 was under development. Was Morgan interested in any of Triumph's new engine range? Morgan, however, demurred politely, explaining that he was dead set on using the Rover V8 – a prescient decision anyway, as it later turned out, given the several reliability problems of the Triumph V8. After more delays, Peter Morgan went to see Sir George Farmer, Rover's chairman, who explained that Morgan would be required to get permission from General Motors to use the Rover power unit. Sir George said he would make the request on Morgan's behalf, which he did, and was very quickly answered, with a 'yes'.

In an effort to hurry the arrangement – it was now October 1967, which was worrying for the future of the Plus 8 – Morgan invited Harry Webster and George Turnbull to Malvern and gave the two BL men a chance to drive the prototype Plus 8. Both were clearly impressed, telling Morgan that the deal was on and deliveries would start in the following April, when the Rover 3500 had launched. This was good news, better than it might at first sound, because it allowed Maurice Owen and Peter Morgan to execute a busy six-month development period on the car and set up the Malvern factory to produce the Plus 8. Maurice Owen was to become a stalwart of the Morgan Motor Company, rising to the long-held position of technical director and a member of the firm's board.

Several improvements to the car followed. The Girling disc/drum braking system was made more powerful and effective with the fitting of a vacuum servo to reduce pedal effort. Windscreen wipers were increased by 50 per cent, becoming a three-blade system, better to clear the narrow rectangle of the glass. The obviously greater consumption of the bigger capacity engine suggested a larger capacity fuel tank, which increased from the Plus 4's 9.2 gallons to 13.6, almost a 50 per cent increase. New to any Morgan car was the replacement of a DC generator with an alternator and the fitting of Lucas LR6 twin spot lamps acting as long-range lamps, plus a hazard-warning setting of the indicator lamps. Besides being a novelty in a Morgan, the latter was a small but useful first, the use of an AC alternator instead of the traditional DC dynamo being a better way to look after the electrical system and charging of the rear-mounted battery. This also helped with the added electrical

Above: Lucas spot lamps increased long-range illumination.

equipment carried then or later on the Plus 8: the three instead of two screen wipers, the spot lamps, and the hazard-warning flashers, amongst other details.

Thus was formed the new Morgan four-wheeler, which was most ambitiously to be the eventual replacement for the Plus 4 – although this did not happen until 2000, when the last Plus 4 was built (the 4/4, available in two- or four-seater versions was not affected). Production at last got under way in 1968, at the eventual rate of around 15 cars per month. It was in such trim that the largest engined of any Morgan to date was launched at the London Motor Show in October that year, from which time both its sales and competition progress advanced healthily.

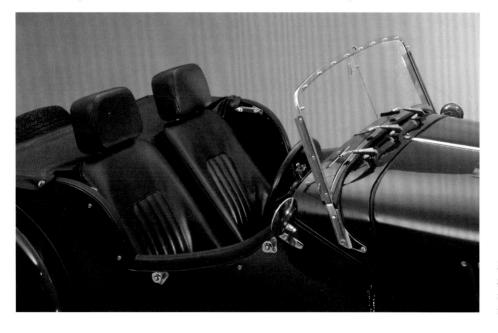

Left: Development showed the need for triple wipers to clear the shallow windscreen.

FIRST DECADE
1968–1978

The Plus 8 goes into production

Two complete Plus 8s, in yellow and blue, plus a polished chassis appeared on the Morgan stand at the 1968 Earls Court Show and attracted considerable interest. The price was £1,155 basic, plus £322 18s 4d British purchase tax, making a total for UK buyers of £1,477 18s 4d.

The Plus 8 became available more widely from the spring of 1969 when a left-hand-drive version went on sale. At the same time, the Malvern company began to offer an aluminium-alloy-bodied version for the competitively-minded, saving 100lb in weight; this also appealed to owners interested in minimising possible rust problems. Not that motor racing was yet a feature of Plus 8 ownership, nor were the motor sport possibilities of this most powerful of Morgans exploited in the first year of this decade, other than through

some participation in the Motor Cycling Club's long-established Land's End, Exeter, and Edinburgh Trials in 1971, where Peter Morgan and his wife Jane got the MCC's Triple Award for top performance on all three events, plus a Team prize for a Plus 8 group in the 1972 MCC Exeter Trial.

Right: A Morgan advertisement for the Plus 8 on display at the 1968 Earls Court Motor Show.

For 1968 a brand new Morgan the +8

Looks like a Morgan should, but now redesigned with a new big heart. Smooth, effortless, safe power from the aluminium V8 motor. Start from a standstill in top gear if you doubt its ability. Leap to the legal limit in a staggering 7.5 seconds when acceleration is needed. That's *real* power. More room, more comfort, more power, more safety—now yours in the Morgan Plus 8. £1475 tax paid. That's *real* value. Enjoy this new experience at your Morgan dealer or write to us. Do it now.

Morgan Motor Company, Malvern Link, Worcestershire. Tel: Malvern 3104.

See the new Plus 8 and the full range of Morgan cars on Motor Show stand No. 127

The Plus 8 takes to the track

Robin Gray was the first of several drivers who started the Plus 8's true motor racing progress in the autumn of 1972. On his first drive in a friend's example of the new car, in a ModSports race at Mallory Park, he finished second after dicing competitively with a Jaguar E-type. In his next drive in the car, at the Rothmans GP at Brands Hatch at the end of September, he was overall winner.

Robin Gray's mount had had a difficult start to its life. Bought by a Lawrencetune customer named Brian Haslam, an ex-Lancaster bomber tail gunner in the Second World War, it was an early Plus 8 which suffered what for most cars would have been a terminal accident when it fell off Mr Haslam's trailer. Haslam took the wreck to Chris Lawrence's premises in Hammersmith in west London, said that he felt he was getting on a bit too much for this sort of car, and presented it to Chris Lawrence.

As Chris Lawrence said: 'It really wasn't badly damaged, just a bit beaten up, so we rebuilt it to become the Lawrencetune car. We got all our tuning equipment from America in those days. The Rover version of what had been a Buick engine was quite an improvement on the original. It was a die-cast engine built with typical American production methods with zero room for manoeuvre as far as people like me were concerned. The die-castings were extremely good but somewhat flimsy, using a minimum amount of material in the usual American engineering fashion – excellent, perfect for the job, but not ideal for tuning. An early racing version over there was used by McLaren in the first of his CanAm cars and we got some of that stuff, like a massive sump casting to hold the block together.

Below: There is no bad view of the Plus 8 but three-quarter front of this superbly proportioned body is one of the best.

Left: Maurice Owen in the prototype Plus 8 about to tackle Hustyn on the 1972 MCC Land's End Trial.

Below left: Peter Morgan's Plus 8, part of a team of three works cars, climbs Bluehills Mine during the 1972 MCC Land's End Trial.

'We built an engine along those lines and got it staying in one piece. What we did do was a very neat inlet manifold for little IDF downdraughts, which actually went under the bonnet. The Plus 8 in standard form went extremely well by the standards of the day and people weren't really interested in making it go any better, unless they were going racing, when you had to do an awful lot to make it

competitive in the class it had to run in.'

Morgan involvement in motor sport began to blossom around this time. The cars were from outside firms mainly – some were way-out modified Plus 8s, which included cars like John Macdonald's supercharged 550bhp Plus 8; he also got involved in a widened Plus 8 powered by a Traco-modified engine, originally aimed at, but not ever running at, Le Mans. This project is described a littler more extensively towards the end of this chapter.

By 1972 enthusiasts modifying the Plus 8 to make it even faster were more plentiful. Typical tweaking-up work included using a four-barrel Holley carburettor in conjunction with a Sig Erson camshaft kit. Besides modified cams to provide more advanced timing and longer valve opening periods, the kit included hydraulic tappets capable of allowing the V8 to rev to 7,000rpm, helped by double valve springs. An Offenhauser inlet manifold plus a Janspeed exhaust manifold further assisted the engine's breathing. The fuel pump was changed to a Bendix pump capable of feeding the modified engine's much greater thirst. Mallory-supplied transistorised ignition in place of the then standard coil electrics gave spark timing to match the modified valve timing via silicone-rubber-covered stainless-steel ignition leads to the special Champion sparking plugs. Suspension modifications typically involved, as a minimum measure, Koni dampers.

Early production changes

On the production front, development of the Plus 8 continued. In 1969 the chassis was widened by 2in, although the 49in front track was not changed. Dual-circuit hydraulics were introduced for the braking system. An early improvement was to the

Above: Closer view of brake servo and the hydraulic dual-circuit brake master cylinder, the latter introduced on 1969 Plus 8s.

Above: With the hood up the Plus 8 looked like a 1930s sports car.

Below: The spare wheel
was mounted uncovered
on the tail. Note the
twin fuel fillers.

OOD 566G

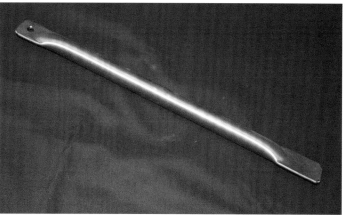

Far left: View under front of 1969 car of triangulating strut added to stabilise front cross-member against the increased twist under braking due to front wheels and tyres larger than on smaller-engined Morgans.

Left: This bottom triangulating stay added to the front suspension cross-frame was a post-1969 modification.

Left: Overhead look at seats and controls of 1969 Plus 8.

front cross-frame that carried the sliding pillar independent front suspension, to stiffen it against the braking vibration mentioned earlier. This was done initially by adding a bottom triangulating stay between the outer part of the bottom of the frame and the chassis to act as a horizontal strut under severe braking load; later, when production got under way properly, larger diameter, thicker-walled tubes were used for the frame itself. Chassis changes in 1970 included the steel floors under the footwells being changed back to wood due to rust problems and a triangular gusset between the bulkhead cross-member and the neighbouring chassis longeron.

In the following year, the engine received the benefit of a tubular four-branch exhaust manifold feeding two downpipes, joined by the balance pipe with its flexible centre section across the front of the V8, with two round-section silencers each side and twin tailpipes with flats on them where they ran close to the wheels.

Minor changes in 1971 included the fitting of anti-burst door locks, covering of the top of the scuttle with crash-absorbent padding in the same finish as the rest of the cockpit interior, and the centre of the steering wheel being changed from a plain hard plastic to a soft rubber one carrying the Morgan name. Also, the

body now sported larger rear lamps placed in horizontal chromed-plastic cylinders, instead of the previous flush-mounted lamps that to some extent faced upwards, as dictated by regulations. Better quality cast 15in diameter wheels with wider 6½in rims replaced the originals.

Within Morgan, there were experiments with an automatic transmission Plus 8, built for Mrs Morgan, mother of Charles Morgan. It was a drophead coupé, with the unusual and old-fashioned feature of rear-hinged doors (to make entry and exit easier). Although, like the four-seater Plus 8 built in the following year, it never went into production, Mrs Morgan kept the car happily well after its prototype days.

Below: Three-quarter rear aspect emphasises the beautifully stable, planted-on-the-road, wheels-at-each-corner-look of the Plus 8.

Far left and left: The flush-mounted rear lamps of the early cars were replaced in 1971 by larger horizontal chromed ones.

Left: This drophead coupé with automatic transmission was a one-off built for Charles Morgan's Mother.

Below: Cockpit and dashboard of 1972 Plus 8 with speedometer in front of passenger.

The Morgan Plus 8 and its rivals in 1968

Make and Model	Top speed	0–60mph	0–100mph	Standing ¼-mile	Fuel consumption	Price inc tax
Jaguar E-type Roadster	140mph	7.4sec	17.1sec	15.0sec	23mpg	£2,117
Lotus Elan S4 SE dhc	124mph	7.8sec	23.3sec	15.9sec	30mph	£1,902
MG MGC roadster	120mph	10.0sec	29.3sec	17.7sec	19mpg	£1,184
Morgan Plus 8	124mph	6.7sec	18.4sec	15.1sec	21mpg	£1,478
Triumph TR5	120mph	8.8sec	28.5sec	16.8sec	24mpg	£1,261
Triumph GT6 Mk2	107mph	10.0sec	39.3sec	17.3sec	28mpg	£1,125
Reliant Scimitar 3-litre	121mph	10.0sec	29.6sec	17.1sec	23mpg	£1,576
Volvo 1800S coupé	107mph	11.9sec	–	18.6sec	25mpg	£1,919

Above: The four-seater Plus 8 that never went into production.

Below: Close-up of combination dial of instruments on 1969 car.

Below right: The 1972 Plus 8 belonging to Barbara Millard, upholsterer at Melvyn Rutter's Morgan restoration works in Hertfordshire.

The Rover gearbox arrives

In 1972 the most significant change was when the Moss gearbox was replaced by the four-speed all-synchromesh gearbox of the Rover 3500S. In fact, as often happened with Morgan changes, there was a considerable overlap in time between the final dropping of the Moss transmission in September and the introduction of the Rover one in March. The Rover gearbox enjoyed a stiffened casing with finned sump, its own oil pump worked off the rear of the layshaft, taper-roller layshaft bearings, and shot-peened teeth.

The new transmission required a slight widening of the chassis longerons – though this was not accompanied by enough widening of the footwells, where there was now less space for the left foot beside the clutch pedal. A benefit of using the Rover unit was that obviously it could be united with the rear of the engine directly, so avoiding the need for the length lost to the Moss box's torque tube, which in turn allowed the V8 to be positioned further back in the car. This move benefited handling balance – already better with the Moss gearbox than in many front-engined sports cars with a weight distribution of 48.1 per cent front, 51.9 per cent rear as weighed with a half-full fuel tank (measured in the *Autocar* Road Test of MMC 11, the second prototype and pre-production car). The shorter engine-gearbox combination also meant the elimination of the short extension shaft contained inside the torque tube, to the benefit of gearbox rotating inertia and thus gearchange quality. A detail noticed by the observant was the replacement of the original single exhaust with a two-pipe one.

Being in effect a part of the rear of the V8, it did however mean that the previous gear lever sprouting into the cockpit directly from the Moss gearbox had to be replaced by a remote control linkage to bring the gear lever within convenient reach again. Compared to the Moss box (which had gear ratios of first 2.97:1, second 1.745:1, third 1.205:1 and top 1.00:1), the Rover box had a wider span, all the intermediate gears being lower: first 3.62:1 (22 per cent lower), second 2.12:1 (21 per cent lower), and third 1.39 (15 per cent lower). However, this was offset by an eight per cent higher-geared final drive of 3.31:1 instead of 3.58:1. This higher gearing was something Morgan had been wanting from its supplier, Salisbury, for the Plus 8 from the beginning, so it was very welcome.

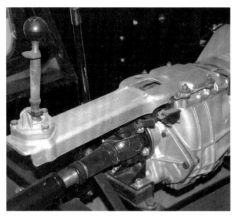

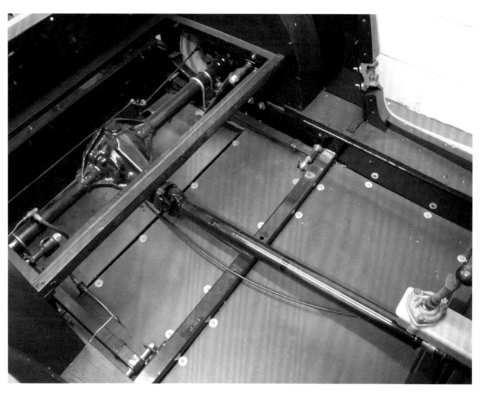

Top left: Remote control for gearchange needed on four-speed Rover gearbox of 1973 Plus 8.

Left: One-piece propeller shaft, differential, rear axle, and one of the rear suspension's two leaf springs on Melvyn Rutter's 1973 Plus 8 under restoration. This demonstrates how the car's low build allows the axle and springs to lie on top of the main chassis.

Far left: The original single-pipe exhaust of the early cars was replaced in 1972 by a twin-pipe one.

Left: The Rover gearbox allowed the V8 engine to be positioned further back.

Cooling and suspension

Also in 1972 there was an increase in radiator core size and a more efficient water pump to avoid the overheating experienced by Plus 8s in hot climates, plus changes in the suspension area.

Morgan had suffered some embarrassing breakages of the front suspension stub axles, which carried the wheel bearings and therefore the wheel, mainly due to poor quality forgings being supplied. So larger diameter stub axles were introduced, which completely avoided the potentially very dangerous problem. Steering arms were also strengthened. During the same period, the rear track was widened, as Mark Aston (former technical director and later assistant managing director to Peter Morgan) says, 'because on the early cars they used to have to squash the exhaust pipes down to clear the wheels at the back – they were literally bolted to the chassis, so you got a lot of vibration. Widening the track gave them the extra clearance down the side of the car to get the exhaust through.'

Wider tracks but less power

In March 1973 the old recirculating heater was replaced by a more modern fresh-air heater with ram-fed air, controllable from the inside the car (which believe it or not was a new feature) and demisting vents for the windscreen. However, the new heater was the now old-fashioned type with a water valve rather than the much more controllable modern air-blending type of temperature control.

An enlargement of the rear track occurred at the same time, which in turn brought with it wider wings and running boards; the car now had 195/70VR-14in tyres. Then in August 1973 the track was widened by 2in in front, to 4ft 3in, and 1in at the back, to 4ft 4in, with 205/70 tyres. Consequently body width increased by 2in to 4ft 11in, with wider front wings.

The facia was redesigned with instruments differently placed and fingertip-operated stalks now graced the steering column. In the same year, Rover had reduced the engine's compression ratio to 9.3:1 and new SU F6 carburettors were fitted, the overall effect of which was a slight reduction of power and torque to 143bhp at 5,000rpm and 202lb ft at 2,700rpm.

Selling abroad

Below: Core of radiator used, special to higher output of Plus 8's V8 3-litre engine compared with the standards of previous smaller-engined Morgans.

On the export front, there was plenty of healthy demand from various markets abroad, which Morgan, in due course, did its best to satisfy with a left-hand-drive Plus 8. Germany in particular was arguably better suited to the Morgan if only because of its almost universally smoother roads, so that it became Morgan's best overseas market. In the early 1970s, the Malvern company did export to North America, following Rover, but the Solihull company's subsequent pull out due to increasingly severe exhaust emissions demands not long afterwards meant that Morgan had to follow suit.

Four years later, in 1977, Morgan was back in the US, thanks to its distributor, Bill Fink of Isis Imports, in California, ironically the strictest state on emissions. He realised that there was a loophole in the regulations allowing liquid petroleum gas (LPG) power for the Plus 8s, a proportion of which were turbocharged. The cars did have to comply with various body and chassis changes – an enlarged windscreen, 5mph bumpers (achieved by fitting Volkswagen hydraulic pistons behind the front bumpers), side-intrusion-resisting reinforcements of the doors and their pillars, and inertia-reel seat belts. The cleaner burning of LPG fuel was a happy situation, of course, for both the manufacturers and the customer, because its relative cleanliness is to the benefit of oil condition in the engine.

Mark Aston joins Morgan

Mark Aston, a long-time, ultimately senior member of the Morgan firm, has contributed much to this book on the Plus 8 and its successor, the Aero 8. He talked to the author about his beginnings with the company as a young man at around this time. 'I went to Morgan in 1976–77 when the last of the four-speed gearboxes went out – the Rover four-speed (which followed the first cars with the Moss box) and then it went to the Rover five-speed.

'I was assistant managing director ultimately, technical director before that – in fact at various times I held most of the senior positions there. I started in the sales office. To cut a long story short, I was approaching finishing at college doing automotive engineering and I started looking for work. At the time I was working for the local Porsche garage and I wrote to all the different manufacturers. I went and saw Aston Martin and a couple or two things at Porsche GB as well, then I got a letter from Peter Morgan saying would you be interested in coming in? Of course, I rang up and he said: "I haven't really got a job at the moment, but I liked your letter – come down and have a bit of a chat, it'll only be a few minutes and obviously if we get something, we can let you know."

'So I went down there three or four weeks later and went in and he came out of his little office, which was on the other side beyond reception and said "Hello," and we had a chat and we talked about Morgan and its history. I knew quite a bit about Morgan before then, being interested. There was a Morgan dealer in Halesowen near our home, Mike Duncan. He had a three-wheeler, which I was fascinated by. He also had a Lotus Twin Cam-engined 4/4, one of the three I think built, quite a nice machine. So I had this interest in Morgans anyway, I'd read a bit about them. So Peter and I got chatting and the half-hour conversation ended three and a half hours later, after a detailed discussion about the prewar GP Mercedes and Auto Unions. At the end of this long conversation, he said: "Well, we haven't really got a job, but you could probably do something in the sales office."

'I was looking for something more in factory management, that sort of thing – engineering – and I said to him: "Well, OK." And he said: "When could you start?" And I said: "Next Monday?" And he said: "Fine."

'So I turned up the next Monday and met the wages person, Anita, who's still there. She didn't know I was coming and Peter Morgan turned up two minutes later – I was there bright and early, obviously – and said: "Look, you need some help in the sales office" – because the sales director was off sick for a while at the time, so the department was not the most organised. One example was that orders for cars were filed in chronological order instead of by names, with no cross-reference alphabetically, so when someone phoned up asking: "Where is the car?", they had to know when they'd ordered it. And at that time, there were a lot of orders – it hit its peak in the late 1970s, early 1980s, but by the mid-1970s they were getting quite a few orders a year more than they were making cars – at the time, production was sort of eight to nine a week.'

Above: A Plus 8 being enjoyed on an open road by an Autocar *driver.*

Left: The Plus 8's centre-hinged bonnet, a relic from an earlier era, was unusual in the 1970s.

Changes in 1974 and 1975

Only minor changes came about in the next two years, such as the replacement in 1974 of the flat fluted-rubber floor covering with wool and nylon carpets in footwells and strips under the seats, and in 1975 a small difference in appearance of the Lucas spot lamps, now with the Lucas lion motif in place of the previous crest. However, this year did see the re-introduction of the aluminium-alloy-bodied Plus 8 in what was called the Sports Lightweight version, aimed at motor sport buyers keen to

compete in production sports car racing. Unlike previous non-standard aluminium-bodied Plus 8s, this car counted (as far as the race regulations were concerned) as a production model, so was now admissible to the race series. The Sports Lightweight Plus 8, which still had a steel bulkhead to retain necessary strength, had wider wheels and tyres and was in fact only produced to the tune of just 19 examples – possibly a fact not too well known to the race organisers.

Above: The revised air cleaners fitted from 1976 fitted under the bonnet without requiring modification.

Revised engine and five speeds

The next year of some notable improvements was 1976. Under the bonnet, the engine became that from the Rover SD1 3500, which was a little more powerful by four bhp at 155bhp (DIN) at 5,000rpm, with maximum torque of 204lb ft at 2,750rpm in spite of a slightly lower compression ratio of 9.25:1 versus 9.35:1 previously. The revised engine's smaller air cleaner avoided the need to modify the housing with a depression to clear the bonnet hinge. Another slight widening of the chassis allowed the power unit to be moved back again, for yet further weight distribution improvement and a little more space in the engine compartment.

The track increased to 4ft 4in at the front and 4ft 5in at the rear.

Taking advantage of the space, a new larger capacity radiator with an integral filler neck was fitted, together with a more efficient water pump, which meant that the previous swirl pot, remote filler and electric fan temperature sensor could all be moved forward on to the new radiator. These changes dealt effectively with the tendency to overheat noted in earlier cars in hot weather.

On the suspension, smaller diameter, Millrace 14 x 6in aluminium alloy wheels were fitted, in place of the previous, original rough-cast 5.5 x 15in wheels.

Right: The wider track introduced in 1976 is evident in this view.

The new Millrace wheels – shod with 205/70VR-14, Dunlop 195VR-14, or optional 195/70VR-14 Michelin XWX tyres – were adopted in October. Also that month, the Rover five-speed gearbox replaced the previous four-speed, with an overdrive ratio fifth (0.79:1), the same fourth (1.00:1) and third (1.39:1), but higher-geared second (2.08:1 instead of 2.13:1) and first (3.32:1 instead of 3.625:1), plus a very marginally higher-geared reverse (3.42:1 instead of 3.43:1).

In 1977 the Plus 8 became the first Morgan with electronic ignition and, to meet new noise regulations, exhaust muffling was improved with an oval-section forward silencer and a round-section rear resonator box. On the body, the originally standard aluminium alloy

Far left: Smaller Millrace 14in aluminium alloy wheel introduced in 1976 could have 205/70VR, 195VR, or 195/70 VR tyres.

Left: At the end of 1976 the Rover five-speed gearbox was fitted.

Left: Aluminium alloy bumpers replaced chromium-plated ones in 1977.

Right: The revised 1977 facia and instrument panel put both speedometer and rev counter in front of the driver.

Far right: Headlamps were fitted with halogen bulbs in 1977.

wings became extras, and were replaced by steel ones, and chromium-plated steel bumpers became aluminium alloy, now fitted to both front and back. A new facia and instrument panel were

fitted, putting the speedometer and rev counter both in front of the driver as well as the supplementary gauges. At the front, headlamps now had halogen bulbs, while the long-range spot lamps

were from Lumax instead of Lucas. The only noticeable changes in 1978 were the availability of 5½in or 6in wide Millrace wheels and the introduction of uprated servo-assisted brakes.

Another Road Test report

Autocar magazine, of which by then the author was technical editor and in charge of the Road Testing team, took the ten years passed since the first test of the Plus 8 (12 September 1968) as a good reason to revisit the car in a full Road Test, then called an *Autotest*. This appeared in the 15 July 1978 issue. The author pulled rank by taking personal charge of this test, using the excellent excuse that he had done the first Road Test, so was best suited to writing this one. That said, the comments had always to reflect the overall feelings and findings of the entire test team, so the verdicts were not just the writer's opinion.

This full production example was fitted with the Rover five-speed transmission. Although the test described it as an overdrive gearbox, in fact in combination with the 3.31:1 final drive and 185VR-15in tyres, the ratios were not ideal. This was obvious from the maximum speeds in the direct fourth and in fifth. Morgan admitted this, Peter Morgan being quoted in the Road Test as saying that he would have preferred to have used the earlier

3.58:1 axle ratio (then no longer available) with the new gearbox, which would have lowered the top gear ratio to provide 24.2mph per 1,000rpm. The car's absolute mean maximum speed of 123mph, which corresponded to 4,700rpm, 550rpm below the peak power speed (5,250rpm), was measured in much worse wind conditions than for the 1968 car and was only just achieved in fifth. In fourth, the Plus 8's mean maximum of 121mph occurred at 5,550rpm, 350rpm over the peak power speed; therefore it was fair to say that fourth and fifth straddled the ideal gear for the true mean maximum.

Otherwise, *Autocar* mostly approved of the choice of intermediate gearbox ratios, which provided change-up speeds of '34, 55, 82, and 115mph, which means progressively decreasing rev drops – nicely spaced for general use, if a little wide for production sports-car racing'. In another respect, the testers thoroughly approved of the Rover gearbox's 'superb gearchange quality – light, precise, short of excess movement, and always a delight

to use, in contrast to the very stiff Moss one. Our only criticism is of the lack of enough spring protection against selecting reverse... There is also totally reliable synchromesh on all forward gears.'

The same thorough approval applied to the performance, described as 'tremendously satisfying. The standing starts were sheer wanton pleasure – drop the clutch in at 3,000rpm, and the limited slip differential encourages both big rear wheels to scream with spin most of the way to that excellent 2.2sec [to] 30mph time. Bang the lever through into 2nd, and there is another yelp as the car leaps forward yet again. Both testers concerned remember faster times in more sophisticated cars, equally but no more exciting than in the Plus 8. It is a Vintage-looking roadgoing dragster.' The engine's effortless 204lb ft of torque, at only 2,750rpm, and 155bhp 'mean magnificent flexibility and super top gear acceleration, with instant pick-up at all times. As before, just for the hell of it, we timed a standing quarter-mile done, with the help of clutch slip up to 7mph (300rpm)

Above left: Frontal view of 1978 Plus 8 Road Test car suggests that wider track.

Above: Peter Morgan at his desk in the Pickersleigh Road Morgan factory in Malvern Link when interviewed by the author for Morgan 60th anniversary **Autocar** *article in 15 July 1978 issue.*

Left: Handling of 1978 Plus 8 **Autocar** *Road Test car being explored by the author.*

solely in the new higher top gear; it took 23.6sec, passing the post at 70mph.' (The proper through-the-gears standing quarter mile figures were 15.1sec at 90mph.)

Under the 'handling and ride' heading, *Autocar* was critical of several aspects. First complaint was about the minimum lock-to-lock diameter of the steering at 39ft 11in. 'It seems paradoxical that a sports car whose purpose is better agility, should have a restricted lock, but it has long been so in this case. Fortunately, the design of the car forces the driver to sit relatively close to the wheel, which helps him provide the muscle needed to steer at low speeds – and indeed at very high ones when cornering.' Steering weight also came in for criticism: 'Steering effort is great enough when rounding a bend at the very high rates of which the car is capable for one to wish that the steering wheel spokes were made smoother near the rim... The weight of the steering makes fast corners excessively hard work, which is a pity because the car's smooth road limit is very high.' Ride was as usual not a good point. The famous Morgan sliding pillar independent suspension allowed 2¾in bump, 1□in rebound, while the movement range of the short half-elliptics was 3¾in bump and 1in rebound. 'The result is an understandably violent ride, which is something else in 1978.'

In spite of this, there was much that the testers loved in the way the car behaved. 'After a while, one takes pleasure in the stirring way the Plus 8 sweeps over open roads – the striding long-leggedness of the gearing and the always confident power allied to the short sharp pitches of the ride together translate into a wonderful bounding motion. But hit a heavier bump at speed, and there is a crash from behind as the axle hits something, you bounce up in the seat – if the hood is up, your head sometimes hits a hood stick   and the car bucks itself briefly askew, wriggling straight again... It must be understood that the Morgan is inherently stable. It has no dangers in its suspension geometry which can build up into something out-of-hand after bump-induced instability.'

The small improvement in overall front cross-frame stiffness was noted with reference to its mildly wayward behaviour ten years earlier. 'The disc/drum servo-assisted layout works well, indeed better than before in our experience, since over 1g is easily achieved at 100lb pedal effort, where previously an annoying stick-slip tyre vibration at the front prevented the car bettering 0.92g at 85lb.' However, curious effects suspected to be connected to the flexibility of the chassis were noted during brake tests. 'Our fade test revealed an interesting manifestation of the flexible chassis. By the eighth ½g stop from 90mph, the pedal effort had stabilised reassuringly at 70lb maximum, 55 per cent higher than at the end of the first stop – the brakes had faded, but not unacceptably, recovering quickly as they should. During the seventh stop, the front wheels began to tramp. During subsequent stops, the tramp would build up so much that one could see the front wheels waggling in sympathy, showing that the chassis was vibrating in twist, presumably due to some cycling variable in the grip of the caliper [pads] on disc when hot.' Interestingly in view of Chris Lawrence's and also Mark Aston's criticisms of the Dunlop tyres used at that time, the test car was fitted with the optional Michelins. 'The Michelin XWX tubed radials grip superbly in wet or dry, and the balance seemed just right.'

Above: A closer look at the dashboard of 1978 car shows that dividing the minor gauges into four small dials on a central panel allows the speedometer and rev counter to be displayed properly in front of the driver.

Right: Looking over author's head at his view of Plus 8 dashboard, bonnet, and road ahead.

That waiting list

On the sales front, to outsiders, Morgan seemed plagued by a shortage of cars to meet demand resulting in long delivery times being quoted by dealers. Mark Aston has some interesting comments on that situation. 'It did get ridiculous. The trouble is, a car of that style became interesting, because there was a big nostalgia mood in the 1970s, and Peter was very reluctant to expand because he'd been through that terrible period in the 1950s when he took over the company from his father and, frankly, the business was on its knees and they were doing sale or return to America on the Plus 4s, so he was very aware of that time and very reluctant to expand, and I totally agreed with him. His view, which proved to be right, was that waiting lists are all theoretical.'

'Various people had waiting lists – Porsche did, Mercedes did – there was a four-year wait to get a 500SL, then 18 months later they're available off the shelf. Morgans didn't go through that period, they stayed fairly stable, but in fact when it came to the crunch, the drop-out rate in the orders was high and a lot of the agents were calculating their waiting lists on the number of orders they got and the number of cars they were getting. And the number of cars they were getting was largely dependent on how effective they were at sending the specifications. That's what I got involved in fairly early on.'

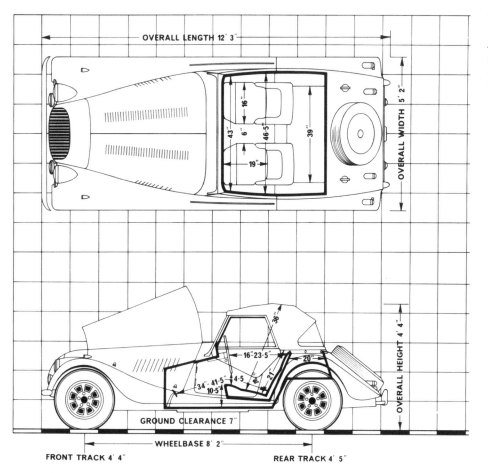

Left: Main dimensions of 1978 Plus 8 with Rover five-speed gearbox, higher-geared, wider track as measured for Autocar Road Test *in 15 July issue.*

Below: Worth waiting for... The Plus 8's classic lines are emphasised by two-tone paintwork.

The Traco Plus 8

The Plus 8 was a great temptation to outside firms and clients interested in motor sport and therefore in variously modified versions of the car. One of the wildest of these, certainly engine-wise, was the Traco Plus 8 mentioned shortly after the start of this chapter, so called because of its Traco-modified Oldsmobile V8 feeding through four Weber 48IDA carburettors. The engine's special split inlet manifold demanded two large cut-outs in the bonnet, fed by a scoop

which, sitting over the normal Morgan bonnet hinge, doubled as a cover for the carburettor intake trumpets; undoing Dzus fasteners permitted the scoop to be removed, necessary to allow a bonnet side to be raised when required. Transmission was provided by a Triumph TR8 rally car gearbox.

Another identifying feature of this car was its width, made so by the fitting of 72-spoke wire wheels with specially made

Rudge-Whitworth hubs with triple spinners and 7in rims in front, with 9in rims at the back. The result was that this particular car was reckoned to be the widest Plus 8 ever seen. Built at Malvern, this bumper-less body was fitted with a trials number plate and a full anti-roll bar. It was intended to run for the Thermal Efficiency Award at Le Mans, but the ACO (the Le Mans organisers) changed the formula for this award, so the car never raced.

Morgan's own racer

A engineer-cum-racing driver called Rob Wells (who was to figure notably later in Morgan Plus 8 racing history) had appeared on the Plus 8 scene in the late 1960s, when he drove an elderly Plus 4 in club races. In 1974 he started a race-preparation firm called Libra Motive, based in Hampstead, and not long after got hold of a lightweight Plus 4 which he again used in club racing. Towards

the end of 1976, he got involved with race preparation of Charles Morgan's Plus 8, the famous MMC 11, which he, Morgan, was planning to race in the ProdSports Championship in the following year. Knowing how his job as a TV cameraman would at times prevent him entering all the Championship races, he said that Wells could drive in other races. Charles Morgan

was in fact away more than he'd planned, so Rob Wells had some useful experience in the more powerful car, in which his talents as an engineer prompted him to notice how it might be improved in various respects. The consequences of this flowered in several different ways in the next decade, covered extensively in the next chapter

The Stapleton competition cars

A couple of other Plus 8 men, as well as the dominant pair of Charles Morgan and Rob Wells, had some success in the 1978–1981

period. They were Bill Wykeham, the driver, and Bruce Stapleton of London Morgan dealers Morris Stapleton, for

whom Wykeham worked. Bruce Stapleton was no mean driver himself and had first taken the wheel of a Morgan whilst at university studying agriculture. The car was a necessarily cheap second-hand one, which he entered in some racing, enjoying the experience enough to neglect his university work so that he lost his place there in 1966. In 1967, in combination with his brother and friend Douglas Morris, he started Morris Stapleton Motors. That led to him acquiring a faster Morgan, the 1959 ex-works Plus-4 of Pip Arnold. The car was endowed with a lightweight aluminium alloy body, providing Bruce with some good racing in marque events.

Later, in 1968, two other competition Plus-4s had joined their stable, one of them the very famous car known thanks to its original registration number as TOK, in which Chris Lawrence with co-driver Richard Shepherd-Barron had won Morgan's greatest ever international competition distinction with a class win in the 24-hour Le Mans race of

Right: The Chris Lawrence/Richard Shepherd Barron Plus 8 takes the chequered flag for a class win at Le Mans in 1962.

1962. Seeking something less usual in sports car motor racing, Bruce Stapleton succeeded in entering both cars in the Mugello endurance race, part of whose course involved some of the ancient Mille Miglia route. They were up against severe competition, such as Porsche 911S entries. Although the Plus-4 Super Sports of Bruce Stapleton and Chris Marshall broke a spring on the bumpy course, Bruce's brother John and his co-driver Richard Lloyd in the ex-Chris Lawrence car finished, coming fourth in their class after those Porsches; a good effort.

Stapleton provided a lightweight Plus 8 for Wykeham to start racing and he did more than well enough to merit being given a better car for the 1977 season, built specially for production sports-car racing, with the latest Rover SD1 V8 that with its larger valves gave more power. The car also benefited from wider-rimmed 14in wheels. However, minor engine bothers with lubrication for a power unit so far unused for competition running messed up several events for Bill.

Consequent development work over the following winter included a fair bit of proper testing, plus more work in turning the SD1 engine into a power unit fit for sports car racing. A typical morning at a circuit started with suspension adjustments to help decide on tyre choice and tyre pressures by putting the car through various test manoeuvres, followed by a general check of the entire car. After a pub lunch, Bill would then put in some fast laps, to confirm the results of the morning's work as well as set a target time for subsequent racing at the circuit used. This thorough and professional approach deservedly bore full fruit in success in the 1978 season. Bill Wykeham went for the BRSCC/Aleybars ProdSports Championship, in which by the end of the 1978 season he had won his class in that Championship. There was happy news for Morgan itself, as Charles Morgan had run in the rival D. B. Motors-sponsored ModSports Championship, which he ended up winning overall; double success for Malvern Link and the Plus 8.

Above: Driving the Morris Stapleton Plus 8, Bill Wykeham won his class in the 1978 BRSCC/ Aleybars ProdSports Championship.

Right: A Plus 8 is crash tested at the Motor Industry Research Association. This is a late 1990s car with airbags, here being deployed.

Crashing for safety

Passive safety – the ability of a car to sustain a crash impact absorbently enough for the car's occupants not to suffer severe injury – was beginning to become a large influence on car design towards the end of the 1970s. I was at the Motor Industry Research Association (MIRA) test facility at Lindley near Nuneaton one day in 1971. For some reason, I had to divert briefly off the test track proper to near the MIRA workshops, including its famous crash safety test facility, and met Peter Morgan coming out of the crash-test shop. He and some of his employees were there to witness the obligatory impact test on the Plus 8, the first it ever had to undergo. He asked if I would care to join them to watch this happen.

I queried at first if he really meant that. Knowing the relative flexibility of the Plus 8 chassis and its famous ash-framed bodywork, I suspected the car would suffer very badly in such a test – particularly in terms of the strength, or lack of it, compared with modern cars, in the cabin area. Peter insisted that I come in and watch. What I had forgotten was

that there was relatively little mass behind the cabin to cause its collapse in a 30mph barrier crash test. The Plus 8 excelled itself in the impact, its collapsing steering column keeping the risk of chest injury to the dummy test driver well within the maximum permitted, so that the car passed the test successfully.

Mark Aston was later involved in Plus 8 safety engineering. 'I did all the 40 per cent offset crash work on the car. Frontal impact is not bad because it spreads the load across the whole car, whereas the 40 per cent impact is offset by that much, but there were two things in the Morgan's favour – it still had a chassis, which is much better than unitary construction because you could fiddle with it much more easily and much more cheaply, and the other thing, of course, is it doesn't involve a ton and a half of weight.' In test form the Plus 8 weight was around 1,985lb.

'The problem we had is it's a very smooth sort of impact on the traditional car [the Plus 8]. Everybody said we'll have to have an airbag on that because of head impact, but I developed this steering

wheel boss with Astrali, the steering wheel suppliers, which was shaped so that it would collapse, so the [driver's] head could hit the steering wheel. It would allow it to crush, so that combined with the collapsing steering column and everything else and being able to spread the load across the front of the car, using the frame front cross-member which collapsed into the front of the engine, it passed.'

'I think we had three goes at it before we passed it on the Plus 8 – the Ministry guys were amazed – then we did side impact. We did one side impact as a preliminary and then we did a certified test and passed it. The modifications needed were relatively small. It was using the strength and tune-ability of the chassis to make it work. It was very good. We stiffened up the bottom stay on the front suspension – you will recall your braking vibration during your road testing – so that instead of it running just under the lip of the chassis, we put an angle bracket on it so that it was going into the side of the chassis.

'We changed the set-up on the chassis a little bit, stiffening it up in a couple of places. That was really all we did. It is the timing of the incident, making sure things happen progressively and then softening of the boss to allow it to collapse properly. When we finished it, the chest loads we got, because the car folds in the way it does, were 30 per cent of the permissible levels, very low, whilst the head impact was within acceptable levels.

'Originally with the Plus 8, in those days the traditional car, it passed the safety test and emissions. Peter Morgan set the target going; we had long conversations, because when I was involved, we were still on UK national level regulations in safety and emissions. He felt that it was too risky to rely on one market because of potential problems with the American market, so he felt that we needed to spread the market as much as possible, which was a very, very sensible policy. But it meant a certain amount of investment in the whole process of emissions and safety and so Morgan went down the route of being a genuine manufacturer, not a typical low volume one.'

Specifications: 1968 Morgan Plus 8

ENGINE

Description
Overhead valve push-rod V8 with aluminium alloy block and pressed in 'dry' cast iron liners, aluminium alloy cross-flow cylinder head. Chain-driven single camshaft in the vee operating two valves per cylinder via short pushrods and hydraulic tappets. Three-ring aluminium alloy pistons, steel connecting rods, and shell bearings. Five-bearing cast iron crankshaft with torsional vibration damper. Electric cooling fan

Capacity
3,528cc (215.3cu in)

Bore and stroke
88.9mm x 71.12mm (3.50in x 2.80in)

Compression ratio
10.5:1

Maximum power
151bhp (DIN) (112.6kW) @ 5,200rpm

Maximum torque
210lb ft (285Nm) @ 2,750rpm

Carburettors
Twin 1½in SU HS6

TRANSMISSION

Gearbox
Moss four speed with synchromesh on top three gears

Ratios
1st	2.97:1
2nd	1.745:1
3rd	1.205:1
Top	1.000:1
Reverse	2.97:1

Clutch
Borg and Beck, 9½in single dry plate

Propshaft
Hardy Spicer, needle roller bearings

Rear axle
Salisbury 7HA hypoid bevel, ratio 3.58:1. Powr-Lok limited slip differential

BRAKES

Front
Girling disc, 11.0in

Rear
Girling drum, 9in x 1¾in

Operation
Girling hydraulic, vacuum servo

Handbrake
Fly-off lever with cable linkage to rear drums

SUSPENSION

Front
Independent. Sliding pillars, coil springs, telescopic dampers

Rear
Half-elliptic springs with live rear axle, lever-arm dampers

STEERING

System type
Cam Gears worm and nut

Number of turns lock to lock
3½

Turning circle
37ft 0in (11.3m)

Steering wheel
Astrali three-spoke, 15in diameter

WHEELS AND TYRES
5½J x 15in cast magnesium alloy wheels

Tyres
185VR-15in Dunlop SP Sport radial ply

PERFORMANCE
Autocar Road Test, 12 September 1968

Top speed
124mph (199kph) hood up
118mph (190kph) hood down

0–50mph (80kph)	5.2sec
0–60mph (96kph)	6.7sec
0–70mph (112kph)	8.6sec
0–80mph (128kph)	11.8sec
0–90mph (144kph)	14.5sec
0–100mph (160kph)	18.4sec
0–110mph (177kph)	25.7sec
Standing quarter mile (402m)	15.1sec

Typical fuel consumption
21mpg (13.4l/100km)

DIMENSIONS

Length
12ft 8in (3,861mm)

Width
4ft 9in (1,448mm)

Height (hood up)
4ft 2in (1,270mm)

Wheelbase
8ft 2in (2,438mm)

Track
Front: 4ft 1in (1,245m)
Rear: 4ft 3in (1,295mm)

Ground clearance
7in (178mm)

Weight
1,979lb (898kg)

SECOND DECADE
1979–1988

Injection and racing successes

At the Geneva Show in March 1979, the Plus 8 appeared with Millrace wheels available with 5½in or 6J rims, with Dunlop 205VR-14in tyres or with Michelin XWX as an option. Wire wheels were not offered on the Plus 8 production cars, thanks as usual to fears about the strength of their hubs. The brakes' vacuum servo was removed. Two years later, carburation changed from the faithful SU HIF6 to Zenith-Stromberg CDEF175 with automatic choke, simply because the Stromberg had been designed to deal with the exhaust emissions standard of the time. Also in 1981, the width of the car gained its final increase to 5ft 3in to accommodate new 15in 6½in-rimmed wheels, using a higher quality wheel casting carrying the Morgan logo. The new wheels were shod with more obviously low-profile Pirelli P6 tyres, in the 205/60VR-15in size. Inside the cockpit, the strips of carpet under the seats became a one-piece carpet each side. Late in that year, in certain markets abroad, the headlamps were supplied by Cibié instead of Lucas. Next year, 1982, a detail difference was changing to two fuse-boxes instead of just one.

Below: With a healthy waiting list Morgan did not need to do much advertising but these are typical. 'A Winning Team' dates from 1981 and 'The professional choice' from 1982.

Modifications for America

The US was not a market officially catered for in Malvern production, simply because the company had been put off in the previous decade by increasingly demanding American passive safety and emissions-reduction regulations. However, Morgan's San Francisco-based importer, Bill Fink, was a dedicated Morgan fan, reportedly equal in his enthusiasm for the marque to that shown by any of his customers. He noted that such regulatory frustrations could be avoided to some extent if the imported car could run on propane in place of its usual gasoline (petrol).

He therefore set himself and his company, Isis Imports Inc, to modifying the engine (a) to use propane and (b) the car's chassis to meet American construction requirements. For the purposes of this book concentrating on the Plus 8 – Mr Fink also applied much of the same to the Plus 4 – the chassis was improved by modifying the sliding pillar front suspension to provide less positive camber. This, of course, was not an American safety demand but it did help front-end grip and thus the car's handling.

On the passive safety front, Bill Fink

fitted some additional structure to the doors to give adequate side-impact protection. He did so by adding what the Americans called hoops of 'rollbar stock' tube on which the door hinges were fitted, plus another piece of stronger frame to stiffen and reinforce the other side of the door frame. Aluminium alloy beams (of the type usual in other cars for anti-intrusion reinforcement) were fitted within the normally ash-framed doors themselves, requiring only marginal cutting away of the ash frame to suit. To give the car the mandatory '5mph' bumpers, Mr Fink's answer was ingenious, taking hydraulic pistons from imported Volkswagen Rabbits (the American market name then for the VW Golf) to fit behind the steel tube doing duty as the bumper beam.

Isis Imports's modifications for the originally Buick-Rover V8 went usefully well beyond simply what was needed to run on propane (or LPG as it more commonly known nowadays), by optionally adding turbocharging. LPG was a good fuel to use, as it brings with it an exceptionally high maximum anti-knock octane value of around 105 octane, so that the V8's 9.4:1 compression ratio did not need to be reduced.

Its other considerable advantage for making the Plus 8 compatible with US exhaust emissions requirements then was that in contrast to gasoline, it is considerably cleaner burning. That meant that no extra emissions control measures were necessary, even with the Rajay turbocharger's 6psi boost, which considerably increased combustion pressures and therefore usually meant retarding the ignition timing in a gasoline-drinking engine. The LPG engine's specification was therefore more than usually in total contrast to what would have been essential with gasoline.

A larger 16 (Imperial) gallon fuel tank was fitted in place of the usual 14-gallon one, the extra size being necessary because contemporary regulations demanded a 20 per cent (by volume) air space in the tank to allow for thermal expansion, reducing the effective fuel volume by around the same proportion. To prepare the LPG for combustion, liquid gas being fed to the engine had to be pre-vaporised, so that a vaporiser heated by the engine's coolant had to be added, mounted on the firewall. Another piece of additional kit was the vacuum-powered fuel lock-cum-filter that kept fuel safely out of the engine when it was switched off.

The twin SU carburettors fitted to the standard engine were replaced by an American Impco LPG carburettor, which included its own automatic mixture enrichment device needed for cold starts. The standard Lucas Opus electronic ignition system was modified slightly to optimise it for propane, as this fuel needs more initial advance of ignition timing. Overall result was the Morgan Plus 8 with what was estimated to be 225bhp (SAE) at 5,000rpm at the turbocharger's 6psi maximum boost, with maximum torque reckoned to be in the area of 240lb ft at 3,000rpm.

ProdSports Championship racing

Turning to the motor sport scene at the start of this decade, we must first continue the story of Rob Wells, whose driving of MMC 11 improved enough for him to win a few races; the progress continued sufficiently for his ability to prosper, so much so that he shared the driving of MMC 11 in the 1979 DB/CCC ProdSports Championship with Charles Morgan. First race of this series was at Thruxton, which he won narrowly ahead of a TVR. The next event he won convincingly and the same occurred at several other events, at which Charles's work at filming in the general election forced him to give the drive to Rob. At a Bentley Drivers' Club event, however, the engine failed in practice whilst Charles Morgan was driving. Happily, Morgan team spirit saved the day for Rob when Bob Stuart lent him his Plus 8 for the Silverstone event in late August, which he won.

Wells now got busy preparing a replacement engine for MMC 11, which was good enough for the car in his hands to win at Mallory Park in September and a week later at Donington, where he set a class lap record. Other successes followed, so that Rob Wells and MMC 11 ended up class-winning in the DB/CCC ProdSports Championship. This turned out to be the second ProdSports class win for MMC 11 that year, a significant one for Rob.

The Stapleton team

In conjunction with Bill Wykeham's Morgan-driving run, Morris Stapleton, the London Morgan dealer, who was mentioned in the previous chapter. Bruce Stapleton gained a good name as the engineer of that partnership and, besides that, was also a successful racing driver. His engineering work was behind the reappearance of Morgan in international sports-car racing in 1979, when Morris

Below: The special Morris Stapleton Plus 8 competing in the Brands Hatch six-hour race in July 1979.

Stapleton entered a special Plus 8 in the Brands Hatch six-hour race in July of that year. The car was specially built for such endurance events by a combination of Malvern and Stapleton with an aluminium alloy body, wide wings to accommodate 9½in wide wheels, a full roll cage, a hardtop, a fast refuelling system capable of accepting a fill-rate of 20 gallons in under ten seconds, and a central jacking system as another aid to fast pit stops. Stapleton was responsible for the preparation of the engine with four twin-choke DCOE Webers, an American competition camshaft, and special Cosworth pistons.

Bruce unfortunately suffered a family loss that prevented him being involved on race day, so he invited Bill Wykeham to take charge of the Stapleton team and its two drivers, Brian Classick and John Spero, who both had some experience of long-distance racing unlike himself. Driving was divided into 100-minute sessions, mainly to minimise any chance of running out of fuel. Apart from the time lost in necessarily changing rear drum brake linings – much slower than changing disc brake pads and made additionally awkward for Stapleton mechanics by the difficulty of handling hot brake shoes at speed – the Morgan distinguished itself against the other much more modern, much faster, mainly turbocharged cars such as Porsche Turbos by finishing 18th overall to the delight of many of the watching spectators.

A spaceframe chassis for ModSports

Rob Wells's successes in the ProdSports Championship bore fruit in a conversation with Peter Morgan at Silverstone. Peter said that he'd love to have a Plus 8 in ModSports racing again (Robin Gray had ceased racing Morgans) and that he could perhaps contribute a car for the job. Rob, excited by the idea, replied that the best way was to start with a clean sheet of paper, to design a car taking maximum advantage of the relatively liberal Modified Sports Car Championship 'formula' with particular reference to suspension, chassis, and engine position.

This resulted in Morgan providing Rob Wells with an engine, gearbox, chassis, rear axle, and aluminium alloy wings. The result was a comprehensively altered car, although it was built with the blessing and full knowledge of the Malvern factory. The engineering challenge to Mr Wells was considerable, in that the car had to meet the modified sports car racing specification rule – yet whilst taking full account of the external resemblance to the standard Plus 8, it had to contrive to be usefully advanced under the skin. For a start, it had a spaceframe chassis, conceived and constructed by Rob Wells and his Hampstead-based Libra Motive company, which first went motor racing in 1980. The multi-tube chassis was, of course, a proper job, even if it was built to reinforce the standard chassis on which it was founded – in observance of the rules. The result was far stiffer in both torsional and beam strength than the ladder-frame, ash and at best aluminium alloy-bodied production car, and much more modern in its suspension.

First came the job of drawing the reinforcing spaceframe superstructure on the original Morgan chassis, as the ModSports regulations then required, endowing it with a respectable torsional stiffness – in great contrast to the unreinforced Morgan original. The engine was moved no less than 18in rearward for a considerably better dynamic balance. The original Morgan front frame was retained, not with the sliding pillar suspension, but an unequal length double wishbone arrangement. At the back, again as the regulations demanded, the live axle had to be kept but in this case with a five-link location arrangement.

Wheels were 13in diameter with 10in rims in front and 13in rims at the back – unprecedented by Morgan standards. The body was among the most remarkable features of the car, being in effect a glass-fibre copy of the ash-framed original, made in one piece, and located by what amounted

Below: Race-modified Plus 8 with roll cage and full harness at a British motor show.

to a hinge at the back of the car. This meant that the entire 200lb weight of bodyshell could be lifted from the front like a very oversized bonnet to give unrivalled access to the mechanicals of the whole machine.

A uniquely strengthened V8, having thicker walls to the cylinder block and a dry sump lubrication system, was provided by a helpful British Leyland Special Tuning. This encouraged Wells to tune the engine heavily with the help of a Holley four-barrel downdraught carburettor, an American camshaft, Weslake cylinder heads, and Cosworth pistons and connecting rods.

During what was left of the 1980 season, Rob Wells proved the race-worthiness of MMC 3 (as the space-frame-reinforced Plus 8 was registered) in ModSports events by setting a new class lap record for the Silverstone Club Circuit of below one minute. In actual races, he noted various alterations that it would be possible to make to improve the car further, which resulted in losing a further near-100lb of surplus weight during the 1980/1981 winter. This was accomplished by changing the windscreen from safety glass to Perspex, and

exchanging the single large rear-mounted radiator with a pair of more thermally efficient lightweight aluminium-alloy-cored ones in front.

The fruits of this work in preparation for the 1981 STP ModSports Championship were 12 class wins in the 17 races involved. After a protest about MMC 3 by a challenging rival, and a counter protest by Rob Wells that resulted in the rival's car being disqualified, the overall Championship was won by Wells, accompanied by five new class lap records to his and MMC 3's credit.

The Snetterton 24-hour race

Going back to 1980, this was the launch year of Britain's own 24-hour sports-car race at Snetterton, the Willhire, in which the Morgan Sports Car Club entered a three-car, six-driver team. Although using a rolling grid start rather than the traditional Le Mans type, the event followed Le Mans timing, beginning at 4pm. Two of the team were the Lindsays,

John and his wife Mary. Mary Lindsay had already made something of a name for herself in six-hour races with her Plus 8, called JEK from its registration letters, which the couple had acquired five years earlier. JEK was an early Plus 8, the 21st in fact. Mary's taste for long-distance racing had been whetted by the six-hour events, making her keen to do the Willhire.

Preparation for this new race was thorough, including such detail as wire-locking bolts to avoid any chance of them loosening through vibration. All three cars were road-based rather than competition-biased, with only one of them arriving on a trailer, so preparation had to be fairly extensive. The club won the support of a team of helpers, totalling around 40, plus

Below: Three Morgans on the grid for the 1980 Willhire 24-hour race at Snetterton. The Libra Motive Plus 8 (2) of Wells/Morgan/Stechman, the Morris Stapleton car (3) driven by Stapleton/Wykeman/Down/Spero, and the Morgan Sports Car Club entry (8) crewed by the Lindsays/Keen/MacDonald/Garland/Duncan. On pole is the Quarters Racing MGB GT. Behind the Morgans are the Team Narborough Ford Capri 3 litre (4) and the Adam MacMillan Racing BMW 3.0Si (5).

Right: The Lindsay team car rounding Bombhole during the 1980 Willhire 24-hour race.

Below: A pit stop for the Morris Stapleton Motors car during the 1980 Willhire at Snetterton.

the spaciousness of a former Second World War Leyland Hippo lorry to take spare parts and service equipment, including gas welding kit, generators, and even scaffolding. The latter was used to create a weatherproof frame for tarpaulins to provide a dry service area. Their overall aim was to finish successfully by avoiding mistakes, in which sensible purpose they all finished. This was due not least to the Lindsay's car, which kept running during some necessary remedial work on the other two Morgans, so that the team achieved third place overall at the end of the 24 hours.

Two other Plus 8s were involved that day in a race for what was known as the Commander's Cup. One was entered by Morris Stapleton Motors with a four-man team made up of Bruce Stapleton, Bill Wykeham, Richard Down, and John Spero. The other was a works team running the faithful MMC 11 with three drivers: Charles Morgan, Rob Wells, and Norman Stechman. This Morgan factory entry was not lucky, MMC 11 suffering from rear axle bother bad enough to force borrowing a substitute axle from father Peter Morgan's car, with which they finished the event. The Morris Stapleton Plus 8 was more happily placed, winning the Commander's Cup.

A second attempt by the Morgan Sports Car Club on the Willhire 24-hours took place in 1981. This time it used just two cars, the Lindsay's faithful JEK and one coming from Mike Robson. The success in 1980 understandably tempted the team to try a little more keenly for a better position. Things did not begin so well – a front wheel came off the Robson car at cruising speed when being used for a holiday trip to France. In the race, matters went well at first, the Lindsay car driven by John Lindsay leading the race for the first 30 minutes. Not so good was a loose cable on the Robson car, which later developed rear axle problems and, by eight o'clock the next morning, a serious oil loss.

In spite of this, the team was then in eighth position, with Mary Lindsay in JEK holding the fort. She had only been driving for 20 minutes when what turned out to be a broken half-shaft caused a back wheel to part company with the car at Coram

Left: Snetterton 1980. The Morris Stapleton Plus 8 is pursued through the Esses by the Colt Lancer of the Hinckley Motors team.

Below: The Morgan works Plus 8 of Charles Morgan, Rob Wells, and Norman Stechman in the Esses at Snetterton during the 1980 Willhire race.

Above: The Lindsay's faithful JEK is pursued through the Esses during the 1981 Willhire 24-hour race by the winning Opel Commodore GS/E of Carrolls Transport, whose team drivers included Andy Rouse, and a Talbot Sunbeam Ti.

Above: The works Plus 8 with distinctive hardtop is pursued through the Esses by the Franklin team Volvo 244GLT during the 1981 Commander's Cup race at Snetterton.

throttle cable breaking. Despite of all these variously nasty frustrations, the team did well to gain sixth place overall.

The Commander's Cup again, however, provided some strong consolation that day, with a second consecutive win for a Morgan in the hands of another team, its members being Francois Duret, Mike Ridley, Malcolm Harrison, and Norman

Stechman. The works car, MMC 11, also lost its right-hand front stub-axle, and therefore a wheel, a little further round the circuit whilst Charles Morgan was driving. Nevertheless, he contrived to drag the car under its own power back to the pits where the stub-axle and wheel were replaced, allowing MMC 11 to finish the event in seventh place.

Racing with Steve Cross

corner, resulting in JEK spinning and ultimately turning over. Mary was lucky that, in spite of being briefly trapped in the inverted Morgan with fuel pouring from the near-full tank, no fire occurred and she was rescued unhurt but badly shaken. The team's manager therefore dispatched Mike Robson's co-driver, David Saunter, in the Robson Plus 8. Unfortunately, he also had a bad smash, so that Mike Robson was given the reserve Plus 8 to finish the race, forgetting about going for the now unobtainable better position but driving to survive, which he did, in spite of a

In production sports-car racing, a new Morgan driver, named Steve Cross, was to appear on the Plus 8 racing scene after Rob Wells and Charles Morgan. His Morgan baptism was in 1976 when he acquired a roadgoing Plus 8, having entered the racing area in a Ginetta that year. The idea of racing a Plus 8 appealed enough for him to write to the factory in 1979 enquiring how feasible it would be for Morgan to supply a ProdSports Plus 8 for him. At first, the response was to suggest modifying his road car by using aluminium alloy wings instead of the standard steel ones and changing the transmission to the five-speed one. However, after Charles Morgan had watched Steve racing and told his colleagues that Cross was both competitive and a potential winner, a racing chassis was built for him. He had to sell both his Ginetta and the

standard Plus 8 to pay for the new car, although he ended up with too little money to afford preparation of his new purchase until the following year, 1980.

Race preparation was executed by Rob Wells, whilst engine preparation including blueprinting and balancing to the tune of 25bhp extra was carried out by Andy Dawson. An added 5bhp was achieved by some carburettor modifications done by a firm local to Steve. The efforts combined well enough for Steve Cross to find himself comfortably in the top-end places in several races. The next step was to obtain some sponsorship, which turned up after his accountant brought along another of his clients, Lyster Oil, as partners, who agreed to sponsor Cross for the 1981 Lucas-CAV Championship. There he encountered the Porsche 911 of Tony Lanfranchi, who

Right: Steve Cross at Brands Hatch in the Lyster Oil-sponsored Plus 8, in which he entered the 1981 Lucas-CAV Championship.

Far right: Donington 1981. Steve Cross in the Lyster Oil Morgan leads TVRs, which he used to race, and the works Plus 8 MMC 11.

proved to be stiff opposition. The German car was faster on the straights but the Plus 8 proved better in braking and cornering. The two fought closely for the entire series, Cross ending up second to Lanfranchi in the class.

This delighted Steve's sponsors, as well as Morgan, so that in the ensuing winter the newest Rover power unit was sent via Hesketh Racing for preparation, returning to Cross with 195bhp. Morgan provided 15in wheels and firmer dampers plus, thanks to experience with racing MMC 11, advice on caster and camber settings. Thus Steve Cross had a more competitive prospect for the 1982 season, which was demonstrated well in the first race at Silverstone. There both Cross, in the lead, and closely challenging fellow Plus 8 contender Malcolm Paul successfully outpaced Lanfranchi in his Porsche, a Lotus Esprit Turbo, and a TVR Tasmin. Despite steep competition from one car in another class right up to the final race of the series, after coming first in a dozen of the 15 races, Steve Cross and his Morgan narrowly won the Lucas-CAV Championship overall by two points.

During that 1982 season, Steve also successfully entered and won some races in a GT series at Donington. This suggested to him and his sponsors that for 1983,

they should concentrate on the Donington GT Championship. During the preceding winter, the car was thoroughly checked and serviced in readiness for this – very effectively as it turned out. Steve Cross won right from the beginning of the season, something he continued to do through nearly all of the series in spite of strong opposition, so that he ended

up winning Class A in the Donington GT Championship. This was in spite of distracting himself for one of the races by seizing an opportunity to enter a Formula Ford 2000 event. He also finished third in the final Championship race for the Morgan. This, together with the effect of the missed race, denied him the position of overall winner.

Snetterton again in 1982–1984

Undaunted by her unpleasant experience in 1981, Mary Lindsay was as enthusiastic as before about entering the 1982 24-hour race at Snetterton. JEK was still under repair, so the Lindsays asked Jim Deacon if they could use his Plus 8, to which he agreed. This machine had been used considerably in shorter races and was not ideally prepared for 24-hour running, so Mary and her brother John Smith did the required work to uprate Jim Deacon's car. Five drivers made up the car's team: besides the Lindsays, there were Mike Duncan, Peter Garland, and Richard Caswell.

The only problem encountered happened when Mike Duncan was driving. What turned out to be the fuel pump started to fail intermittently, then failed apparently permanently round the other side of the circuit from the pits. Rules

specified that in any forced stop away from the pits, the driver must repair any failure using tools and spares on board his mount. However, the regulations did not forbid the use of two-way radios, which the team had fitted, so Duncan summoned the team, members of which came to the other side of the fence where he had contrived to stop. Here the reason for the engine cutting out was discovered by knocking the fuel pump back into life (a trick familiar to clued-up drivers of other road cars fitted with SU electric fuel pumps). Thus Duncan was able to return to the pits for a replacement pump to be fitted and continued to the finish and a tenth place.

However, it was the faithful old MMC 11 that saved the day, or rather that particular 1982 24 hours. Driven by Rob Wells, Malcolm Paul, and Chris Alford,

Far left: Sponsors of the 1982 Bulldog Morgans team.

Left: Front row of the grid for the 1981 Willhire 24-hour race. On pole is the Carrolls Transport/ICS team Opel Commodore GS/E, which won in 1981. Alongside it is the works Plus 8 of Rob Wells/Chris Alford/ Malcolm Paul.

Above: Jim Deacon's Plus 8, used by the Lindsay team at Snetterton in 1982, is followed through Bombhole/Coram Curve by the Triumph Dolomite Sprint of the Ian Hunter team.

Below: Norman Stechman's Plus 8 leaving the pits towards the end of the 1983 Willhire race.

Above right: Works Plus 8 MMC 11 saved the day for Morgan in the 1982 Willhire 24-hour race and set a new record for the number of laps covered in the event.

Right: Norman Stechman's Plus 8, sponsored by Allied Rubber Products, leads a Ford Capri in the 1983 Willhire 24-hour race at Snetterton.

MMC 11 was in the lead from the second hour all the way, holding that position more and more certainly as the race wore on. It went on to an overall win and a new record number of laps for the event – 970. Morgan secured the Commander's Cup for the third time.

The following year, just two Morgan teams made the 1983 event: Norman Stechman's car, sponsored by Allied Rubber Products, and the faithful Bulldog Morgan team. Mary Lindsay again asked Jim Deacon if he could lend his Plus 8, as the Lindsay's JEK was still off the road being repaired. Deacon was keen to fit a new, more powerful engine but the

Right: The Lindsays'
old faithful JEK
leads a VW Scirocco
through the Esses at
Snetterton in the 1984
24-hour race.

Below: The Wells/
Alford/Morgan Plus 8
does battle with a Ford
Capri 2.8i through
Riches corner in the
1984 Willhire event.

Lindsays said they'd prefer the tried and tested existing one. This turned out to be a good idea as, from occupying 14th position early in the event, the car finished fifth, nine places ahead of the Stechman car.

For the 1984 Snetterton 24-hour race, JEK was at last ready. In spite of its age and the distance it had covered – 16 years and 97,000 miles – and a final drive pinion seal failure, which cost the Bulldog team half an hour lost, JEK finished 12th out of the record 36 starters, which included three Porsche 911 entries that the Morgan beat. Going back to the Saturday/Sunday night, MMC 11 driven by the Rob Wells, Chris Alford, and Charles Morgan team had achieved the lead. Brake bothers put the car back to second but then a broken alternator connection led to battery failure and retirement. That was a great shame for both the car and its drivers, because this 1984 event turned out to be the last Snetterton 24-hour race for which the Plus 8 or any other open sports car was eligible, the race being turned over solely to saloons for 1985.

Morgan Plus 8 and its rivals in 1983

Make and Model	Top speed	0–60mph	0–100mph	Standing ¼-mile	Fuel consumption	Price inc tax
AC 300ME coupé	120mph	8.5sec	26.3sec	16.3sec	21mpg	£11,300
Caterham Super 7 TC	103mph	6.5sec	29.9sec	15.0sec	28mpg	£6,884
Alfa Romeo GTV6	130mph	8.8sec	24.3sec	16.7sec	26mpg	£10,250
Audi Coupé GT Injection	120mph	8.8sec	25.0sec	16.9sec	28mpg	£9,172
Lotus Esprit S3	134mph	6.7sec	20.9sec	15.5sec	23mpg	£15,380
Morgan Plus 8	123mph	6.5sec	20.2sec	15.1sec	22mpg	£10,496
Panther Kallista 2.8	108mph	7.8sec	34.8sec	16.1sec	27mpg	£6,800
TVR Tasmin convertible	124mph	7.8sec	25.3sec	16.2sec	23mpg	£12,744
Porsche 924 5-speed	126mph	9.5sec	29.1sec	17.1sec	28mpg	£10,793
Porsche 944 Lux	137mph	7.4sec	21.0sec	15.6sec	29mpg	£14,462

reprofiled inlet ports for better gas flow and a higher (9.75:1) compression ratio, the injection engine turned out 192bhp (DIN) at 5,250rpm, with torque peaking at 220lb ft at 4,000rpm; this was 2bhp better than the output quoted for the Rover Vitesse, the small improvement being credited to the more efficient exhaust manifold in the Morgan. Finding space for items added as part of the change to fuel injection was no mean task, things like the electronic engine control unit ending up being attached to the body's ash frame.

This move also spelt the end of a large proportion of the engine tinkering beloved of many mechanically minded owners. However, for the moment the move to electronic fuel injection did reverse the regrettable decline in engine performance. This was caused mostly by exhaust emissions regulations and the loss of so-called five-star 100RM petrol, but also because of changes in the requirements for different, stricter standards of power measurement during this period. From the first car's healthy 160bhp net, power had fallen to 151bhp under the German DIN standard, and to a minimum of 143bhp in 1973, when the least performing Plus 8s were sold; with the coming of Rover's SD1 model in 1976, power had recovered a little to 155bhp.

Above: The prototype fuel-injected Plus 8 raced by Charles Morgan

Fuel injection brings more power

At the end of 1983, Rover having moved to Lucas/Bosch LE fuel injection for the engine in the Vitesse, back at Malvern Morgan naturally followed suit, though initially in prototype form, originally sold as a higher-priced car. Thanks also to

Right: The fuel-injected version of the Rover V8 engine.

Far right: A 1985 advertisement for the fuel-injected Plus 8.

Rack and pinion steering arrives

A significant advance in the car's steering in 1984 was the replacement of the worm and nut steering box (supplier Cam Gears having gone out of business) with a rack and pinion box supplied by racing-transmission manufacturers Jack Knight, initially as an option. This was somewhat lower-geared, demanding 3.4 instead of 2.4 turns lock to lock, to the benefit of steering effort in this always non-power-assisted system, something unfailingly complained about when parking a Plus 8. However, the lower gearing apparently did reduce steering 'feel' to some extent as well as reducing the potentially better response usually concomitant with rack and pinion's greater mechanical directness. This was a curious fact, given the considerably improved accuracy and response of the steering to be expected when replacing a worm and nut system, which in the Plus 8 was noted as exhibiting around 2in of steering wheel play measured at the rim around the straight-ahead. The rack and pinion system included the replacement of the former traditional long single track rod with two steering arms pivoting from the centre of the rack, which was said virtually to eliminate the previous model's marked tendency to bump-steer.

The new steering arrangement also brought with it a rather smaller minimum turning circle, reduced from the original Plus 8's near 40ft mean diameter between kerbs to circa 36ft average, to the benefit of manoeuvring. Also, a detail change to the wheelarches removed the long-deplored tendency of the car to rub tyres on the chassis in hard cornering.

At the front of the Plus 8, the Lumax long range spot lamps were changed to Marchal ones and, at the back, a reversing lamp became standard, plus twin rear fog-guard lamps placed on the sloping rear panel.

Above left: Left-hand-drive chassis showing rack and pinion steering newly introduced to replace previous system.

Above: Charles and Peter Morgan.

Charles Morgan joins the family firm

Charles Morgan, grandson of the founder of the company, H. F. S. Morgan, became operationally part of the firm in this decade. As he tells the tale: 'I joined the company in 1985 – and my father Peter and I worked closely together for nearly 20 years up to his death in 2004. We worked together and I think complemented each other; in our case, the father-son relationship worked really very well, basically because the company, certainly through the 1990s, was financially sound – probably more so than it's ever been. Just like the 911, the Plus 8 was an icon; selling very well, it had a 37-year product life, from 1968 to 2004.'

'The thing is that [Plus 8] was very much my father's baby. I believe it was a great car too and as a result of constant development and because the initial idea had been intelligent and quite elegant, that's what gave it its 37-year life. The thing is that it differed from other examples of that trend – the fashion for putting a big V8 in a lightweight chassis – in the fact that the V8 was at the time anyway, 3½ litres. It has its critics obviously but it was the lightest, so it wasn't a big Ford or big Chevy and, of course, the Morgan chassis suited it. It was well back near the centre of the car, so it didn't have that nasty snake-like feeling that the Sunbeam Tiger did, with its big Ford engine over the front axle – or the AC Cobra, which is much front heavier.'

The choice of colours

The Plus 8 was offered with a range of standard colours: Connaught Green, Corsa Red, Indigo Blue, Black, or Royal Ivory. The wing beading could be either black or cream. Special colours, metallic finishes, or two-colour paintwork could be supplied at extra cost to personalise a car.

Improvements for 1986 and 1987

In August 1986, the Jack Knight rack and pinion steering became standard, with the option of a smaller 14in steering wheel in the cockpit, where the warning lamp cluster in front of the steering wheel changed in layout to separate lamps in a T-formation. Late that year, a Land Rover cast-iron exhaust manifold was adopted, with a twin tubular balance pipe arrangement across the front of the engine running out through the left-hand inner wing to a spring-secured balljoint. The exhaust pipe, now a single-pipe one, had three silencer boxes in series, front and back ones being round section and the middle one a lengthy oval section, needed to meet new tighter noise rules. The 205/60VR-15in tyres fitted were now from Avon.

On the quality front around this time, the factory incorporated a number of finishing improvements. Epoxy powder coating was introduced and the long overdue demand for better rust protection was at last met by the coming of galvanising (zinc-coating of steel parts in the chassis). Other corrosion protection was gained by the use of the passivation process for fasteners such as nuts and bolts. Paint quality was improved by spraying the wings while still separate from the body, allowing better paint access to all parts of the wings. The body's long-famous ash frame was better guarded against decay of any sort by the use of Cuprinol dipping. Flooring to carry the fuel tank, originally a steel one, changed to a thick piece of wood. On the equipment front, the twin rear fog-guard lamps mounted on the rear panel were reduced to a single lamp on the offside of the back bumper.

During 1987 the steering wheel changed

Below: A 1986 Plus 8 being cornered enthusiastically.

Prices for export markets

Morgan's April 1987 price list for overseas markets and left-hand-drive cars listed the options available when included in the specification of a new car. They were available for UK buyers too, but they had to pay car tax and VAT on the completed vehicle, of course, the prices below being without those taxes.

Plus 8 petrol injection	£13,135.00
Extras	
Leather upholstery (black or colour)	£435.00
Reclining and folding seats	£110.00
Luggage carrier	£80.00
Door handles	£30.00
Bonnet strap	£22.50
Underbody sealing	£57.70
Rustproofing (Terotex system)	£100.00
Aluminium body and wings	£275.00
Dual tone paintwork	£200.00
Special paint colours	£50.00
Coloured hood, sidescreens, and tonneau	£100.00
Spare wheel cover	£32.50
Headrests	£77.50

Autocar tests the 3.6 injection

to a more readily collapsible type in the interests of passive safety, with a centre pad returning to a black plastic surround to the Morgan name, which was in red against a black background. A tiny detail difference outside was the replacement of the previously chromium-plated cylinders of the rear lamps with body-coloured painted ones.

The fuel injection, rack-and-pinion-steering 3.6-litre Plus 8 was the subject of what the magazine called a Test Update in *Autocar* of 11 March 1987 and the Road Test team's comments reflect, in spite of the standards of the time, an underlying kindling of enthusiasm. 'There have been many changes over the years to the mechanicals and drive train, but the Morgans of today still look the part; a pre-World War II car, the real thing. There are quite a few other small manufacturers who have jumped on the bandwagon in recent years but none has managed to ascend to the Morgan pinnacle.

'We last tested a Plus 8 in 1978, but we did not need an excuse to reacquaint ourselves; if we had, the fact that the Plus 8 is now powered by the fuel-injected 3,528cc Rover V8 would have been reason enough.'

The Test Update went on to admit: 'Aerodynamics, or to be more precise,

a lack of them, play a large part in determining the Plus 8's maximum speed. The effects can be felt as 100mph is reached, and at 120mph there is a definite feeling that the Morgan is beginning to struggle.' However, *Autocar* went on to make it clear that 'maximum speed, however, is fairly academic for the Plus 8 as it is not the *raison d'être* of the car.' The substantial power increase brought by fuel injection 'raises the Plus 8 into the rarefied atmosphere of the supercar in terms of out-and-out performance. A power-to-weight ratio of 178bhp/ton as tested is a mouth-watering figure to conjure with, and one which will stifle the mutterings of any car enthusiast.

'...Where the Morgan really shows its mettle is in the in-gear and standing-start acceleration times. The incremental times in each gear demonstrate admirably the

Far left: The twin rear fog guard lamps were replaced by a single one mounted on the bumper in 1986 and the following year the rear lamps' cylinders became body colour.

Left: Cockpit and dashboard of a 1986 Plus 8.

flexibility of the Rover V8 engine, and 3.4secs to go from 50–70mph in third gear is not to be sniffed at...

'Despite the age of the design, the Plus 8 manages to gain an enormous amount of traction off the line, helped in no small way by the limited slip differential, and the low-profile 205/60R 15in tyres. The main problem off the line is wheelspin but with a bit of practice this can be brought under control and used to launch the car most effectively. It is not often that we test a two-wheel-drive car which reaches 30mph in 2secs from a standing start.

'The benchmark 60mph comes up in an impressive 5.6secs in second gear, with the quarter-mile post reached in 14secs – eat your heart out, GTI drivers.'

There was predictable criticism of the ride as 'diabolical'. 'The decrepit state of British roads – motorways included – does not help, but hit a bump, even a small one, at speed and there is bump steer as the front goes over it and then a resounding crash from the rear axle. The driver is thrown sharply upwards and if the hood is up there is a tendency for the top of your head to make contact with one of the hood sticks. Look down the long bonnet line of the Plus 8 on the motorway, and the motion of the front end bears a strong resemblance to the nose of a bloodhound on the trail – constantly moving from side to side. Because of the bouncing tendency it is a handful when driven hard down a country road but not dangerous by any means because the Plus 8 is a very stable car and will always put itself right. But the driver has to work hard.'

The sheer pleasure of driving a Plus 8 shines through, nevertheless. 'In a lot of ways, however, it is this side of the Morgan's character which probably appeals to owners in this pampered age of power steering and boat-like ride.'

The new steering gained approval. 'Rack and pinion steering is now standard, and with 3.4 turns lock-to-lock,' versus 2.4 for the former Cam Gears worm and nut steering, 'it is far more manageable, if still on the heavy side.'

So also did the handling. 'Driven hard into a tight corner, the Plus 8... understeers heavily. Being so close to the steering

wheel gives the driver sufficient leverage to control the car, but be warned: if nothing else, Morgan driving builds up the chest and shoulder muscles.' However, the report continued: 'Back off the throttle on entering a corner, and the understeer disappears to be replaced by oversteer. The back end swings out of line and can then be caught on the throttle to power the Plus 8 round a corner in a most satisfying way.

'Despite the antiquated chassis and

suspension design, the Morgan Plus 8 is a joy to drive as far as handling is concerned and no matter what people say it is ultimately safe.'

The test's last paragraph sums up the undeniable appeal of the Plus 8. 'It is by no means a car which everyone will like. It is for those people who really enjoy the pleasures of seat-of-the-pants motoring, and who are bored with the mass-produced boxes so often seen on the roads today.

Above: The now fuel-injected Plus 8 tested by Autocar *in 1987 was among the fastest accelerating sports cars of its time with 0–60mph in 5.6sec.*

Opposite: Autocar's *1987 Test Extra Plus 8 in a dramatic contre jour shot.*

Left: The 1987 Plus 8 with rack and pinion steering was described by Autocar *as 'far more manageable'.*

Morgan Plus 8 and its rivals in 1987

Make and Model	Top speed	0–60mph	0–100mph	Standing ¼-mile	Fuel consumption	Price inc tax
Audi Coupé GT 2.2	122mph	8.8sec	26.1sec	16.5sec	30mpg	£13,855
Caterham 1700 SS	111mph	5.6sec	19.9sec	14.6sec	26mpg	£8,700
Jaguar XJ-S 3.6 Cabriolet	141mph	7.4sec	19.7sec	15.9sec	19mpg	£23,700
Mazda RX-7	134mph	8.5sec	23.2sec	16.2sec	21mpg	£15,250
Morgan Plus 8	122mph	5.6sec	16.4sec	14.4sec	23mpg	£15,436
Naylor TF 1700	89mph	12.5sec	–	19.5sec	29mpg	£14,949
Panther Kallista 2.8i	109mph	7.7sec	30.5sec	16.3sec	23mpg	£10,750
Porsche 924S	133mph	8.2sec	20.9sec	16.1sec	28mpg	£18,464
Toyota MR2 T-bar	119mph	7.7sec	25.0sec	16.5sec	32mpg	£11,999
TVR Taimar 350i	136mph	6.6sec	20.2sec	14.8sec	22mpg	£17,865

Changes in 1988

During this decade, the Morgan Motor Co followed then-current environmental thinking in the motor industry in deciding to modernise its paint shop. This involved changing to water-based paints, in place of the traditional solvent-based systems. There was no deleterious effect on finish and paint quality but the process was much cleaner and less harmful to the atmosphere. On another practical front, underbody sealing was provided in 1988 as standard, instead of an option as it had been previously. Inside the car, the heater was improved a little with the introduction of better control.

This year brought a detail change to the cast aluminium alloy wheels, which in the process of changing back to Pirelli P6 205/60VR-15 tyres, became ½in shallower. Other tyre makes used around this time included Uniroyal and Avon.

True, the modern car is a sophisticated and ultimately competent piece of machinery, but despite the fact that there really is no excuse for the atrocious ride of a Morgan Plus 8, it wins hands down in terms of character, performance and sheer driving pleasure. A car which really separates the men from the boys.'

Left: Another dramatic photo of **Autocar's** *1987 Road Test Plus 8, under the Severn Bridge.*

Below: The 1988 change to water-based paints did not affect the quality of finish.

Right: Shallower alloy wheels resulted in the change back to 205/60VR-15 tyres in 1988.

Specifications: Morgan Plus 8 Injection

ENGINE

Description
Overhead valve push-rod V8 with aluminium alloy block and pressed in 'dry' cast iron liners, aluminium alloy cross-flow cylinder head. Chain-driven single camshaft in the vee operating two valves per cylinder via short pushrods and hydraulic tappets. Three-ring aluminium alloy pistons, steel connecting rods, and shell bearings. Five-bearing cast iron crankshaft with torsional vibration damper. Electric cooling fan

Capacity
3,528cc (215.3cu in)

Bore and stroke
88.9mm x 71.12mm (3.50in x 2.80in)

Compression ratio
9.75:1

Maximum power
192bhp (DIN) (143kW) @ 5,250rpm

Maximum torque
220lb ft (298.5Nm) @ 4,000rpm

Fuelling
Lucas/Bosch LE fuel injection

TRANSMISSION

Gearbox
Rover five speed all synchromesh

Ratios
1st	3.32:1
2nd	2.08:1
3rd	1.39:1
4th	1.00:1
Top	0.83:1
Reverse	3.42:1

Clutch
Borg and Beck, 9½in single dry plate

Propshaft
Hardy Spicer, needle roller bearings

Rear axle
Salisbury hypoid bevel, ratio 3.31:1. Powr-Lok limited slip differential

BRAKES

Front
Girling disc, 11.0in

Rear
Girling drum, 9in x 1¾in

Operation
Girling dual circuit hydraulic

Handbrake
Fly-off lever with cable linkage to rear drums

SUSPENSION

Front
Independent. Sliding pillars, coil springs, telescopic dampers

Rear
Half-elliptic springs with live rear axle, lever-arm dampers

STEERING

System type
Jack Knight rack and pinion, collapsible column

Number of turns lock to lock
3¼ (3½ with 14in wheel)

Turning circle
36ft (11m)

Steering wheel
Astrali three-spoke, 15in (optional 14in) diameter

WHEELS AND TYRES
6½J x 15in cast aluminium alloy wheels

Tyres
205/60VR-15in Avon radial ply

PERFORMANCE
Autocar test extra, 11 March 1987

Top speed
122mph (196kph)	
0–50mph (80kph)	4.3sec
0–60mph (96kph)	5.6sec
0–70mph (112kph)	7.9sec
0–80mph (128kph)	9.7sec
0–90mph (144kph)	12.3sec
0–100mph (160kph)	16.4sec
0–110mph (177kph)	21.3sec
Standing quarter mile (402m)	14.4sec

Typical fuel consumption
23mpg (12.3l/100km)

DIMENSIONS

Length
13ft 0in (3,962mm)

Width
5ft 3in (1,600mm)

Height (hood up)
4ft 4in (1,321mm)

Wheelbase
8ft 2in (2,438mm)

Track
Front: 4ft 5in (1,346m)
Rear: 4ft 6in (1,372mm)

Ground clearance
6in (152mm)

Weight
2,022lb (917kg)

THIRD AND FOURTH DECADES
1989-2008

Final changes for the Plus 8, Roadster V6 arrives

The late 1980s were mostly a lean period for major advances in the Plus 8's story. Typical was 1989 with the arrival of a walnut veneered dashboard, which offered something radical for any Morgan, if not for most cars, with an optional lockable glovebox. Instruments bore a new logo, of the Tudor concern, which by then had taken over Smiths Industries. A battery isolator switch was set on the heelboard between the seats and the adoption of Continental pattern fuses meant that they were housed in a single longer fuse-box under the dashboard. Outside the car, the rear lamps and indicator lamps swapped places.

A comparison test with a BMW M3

The 8 February 1989 issue of *Autocar & Motor*, as the magazine was then known, carried a pretty extraordinary comparison drive article by Andrew Frankel on the Morgan Plus 8 and, of all cars, the convertible version of the vastly more modern and wildly different BMW M3. Two more diverse vehicles it would be hard to imagine but the Morgan came through this surprisingly well, though (as one might surmise) not by any means in all respects. It was, on smooth roads, impressively fast, thanks to the combination of its 190bhp from the 3.6-litre Rover V8 and a kerb weight of 2,022lb, whereas the 200bhp of the BMW's 2.3-litre straight six had 3,105lb to contend with. In laden one-up power-to-weight-ratio figures, those equated to the Plus 8 enjoying 194bhp/ton laden, 50bhp per ton more than the M3's 144. In terms of maximum torque, the 53 per cent larger capacity of the older-specification Rover V8 exceeded that of the BMW engine, to the tune of 220lb ft at 4,000rpm to the BMW's 177lb ft at 4,750rpm, a 24 per cent difference.

So in acceleration both from a standing start and from one speed to another up to circa 100mph, the Morgan was quicker: 0–60mph was done by the Plus 8 in 5.6sec and in 6.0sec by the M3; 0–100mph in 16.4sec (Morgan) against 16.6sec (BMW). However, as the widely different drag of each car began to tell, the gap was closing, so that for 0–120mph the situation was reversed as the M3's conspicuously better aerodynamic drag figure showed its advantages over the obviously much higher drag of the Plus 8 – the M3 doing 0–120mph in 28.3sec, 1.3sec faster than the Plus 8. Then, running on to maximum speed, the BMW kept climbing to peak at 144mph to the Morgan's 122mph.

In cornering and handling, the BMW mostly was far on top. To quote Mr Frankel: 'The BMW waits until the corners before it seduces you. The M3 has as good a claim as any to having the most competent *and* entertaining front-engined chassis in production. Remarkably, the convertible has lost none of the saloon's ability. Turn-in is sharp and the grip from the 225-section Michelin MXX tyres is of the very highest order.

'The convertible will understeer or oversteer on demand, but its basic cornering stance is one of strong neutrality. Push on harder and it just feels better and better, neutral cornering balance eventually giving way to mild, benign oversteer. The steering, so full of feel, lets you keep the front wheels pointing in the desired direction, without drastic correction, and the car follows this line faithfully. It has no hidden vices, no ghastly secrets.'

'Driving the same road in the Morgan induces acute culture shock. Grip is not the problem if the road is smooth. With only 2,000lb to persuade to change

Left: Dashboard and controls, including safety-orientated rocker switches.

Below left: What the driver sees in front of him, including a Morgan-badged steering wheel.

Below: In 1989 the rear lamps and indicators swapped places.

Below: The traditional louvred bonnet with its central hinge is highlighted in this view.

direction, the 205-section Uniroyals allow the +8 to be hustled through well-surfaced corners at a cracking pace. Put it on the pockmarked B roads of the Lake District and the story is very different. The car hops wholesale across the road as soon as look at a bump. The ride is truly appalling.

'And the otherwise dead steering can generate the sort of kickback that wrenches the wheel from your hands. You drive this car from the seat of your pants. Do this, and it is not without its rewards. Fight the steering, kill the heavy understeer with a bootful of throttle, be ready to catch the inevitable tail slide, and

you will have one of the most invigorating rides this side of a rollercoaster. Despite the dead steering, the Morgan can be placed accurately, but it takes practice.'

Naturally, on the practical side, the BMW's power-operated hood puts it in a different league of convenience compared with the Morgan and something of the same was said about driving each car with the hood raised. Up to 70mph, the M3 feels and sounds like its saloon brother, road and engine noise overcoming what wind noise is present; above that speed, there was some wind roar, but it was described as 'well suppressed'. In contrast, *Autocar &*

Motor's man did not recommend hood-up driving in the Morgan at motorway speeds. 'The tall gearing keeps engine noise to a minimum but since the wind drowns any attempt to hear anything, it's rather academic. The wind causes the hood to billow skywards – creating some much needed headroom – and assaulting you from every hole in the ill-fitting side-screens.'

Nevertheless, the Plus 8 mitigated its failings in several ways. 'The Morgan does do some practical jobs surprisingly well. The seats are comfortable even if the ride is not. The two-stage heater keeps you warm in freezing conditions.

Opposite: The 190bhp 3.6-litre V8 with its fuel injection system partly visible in this view.

Above: Hood erected, displaying less than ideal three-quarter rear view.

Right: The hood itself is separate from the hood sticks, which are secured by straps when the top is lowered.

Top right: Detail of sidescreen with its sliding Perspex windows.

Below: A 1989 car from a low angle showing off its wheels.

Opposite: Seats for driver and passenger have some side support.

The driving position is not terrible, even if it is short on leg room.' Perhaps remarkably, both cars got praise for the quality of their build.

'Both cars are beautifully built. Scuttle shake, which can reduce a sound saloon into a rattling undesirable, is only apparent in the BMW on badly broken surfaces. Paintwork is deep and lustrous, and body panels fit tightly and evenly.

'If anything, the Morgan is more impressive. The test car was Morgan's demonstrator and even after 40,000 miles of the suspension trying to shake the car to pieces, it still felt and looked like new, apart from the odd stone chip. Drive one and you will know that this is no mean achievement.' That 40,000 miles was about three times more than most manufacturers' press demonstrators accrued, both then and now.

So, in spite of its several failings, the Morgan gets more votes for its fun and character in this extraordinary comparison. 'What it offers is an unrivalled tactile experience. You can get out of the BMW, unruffled, after a hard blast down a fell road and marvel at the car's ability. Do the same in the Morgan, and you get out with a real sense of achievement.

'Then there is the way the car looks. Beside the Morgan the BMW, for all its flared arches and spoilers, looks anonymous. The Morgan looks classically

Below: Classic profile of a 1989 Plus 8 reveals the exhaust run.

beautiful. It has a hint of fragility that makes you want to look after it. For all the money it costs, the BMW is much less of an individual.'

'The Morgan has only one real problem. It is pointless driving it in anything but ideal conditions. The car's comprehensive inability to transport its occupants for long distances in anything but severe discomfort is something that only the most die-hard nut will discount. But when the roads are dry and the sun shines, you cannot have too much of it. The Morgan ladles out fun like the BMW never could.

'The essence of it is that in the BMW you enjoy the car, while in the Morgan you enjoy yourself.'

Left: Three-quarter rear view suggests a car eager to accelerate powerfully.

Catalytic converters and the 4-litre engine

Continuing the evolution of the Plus 8, June 1990 was more interesting, with the introduction of the 94 x 71mm bore and stroke 3,946cc Rover V8 power unit. With its fully mapped hot-wire sensor fuel injection, the engine produced 190bhp at 4,750rpm and 230lb ft of torque at 2,600rpm. This was not quite what the enlarged capacity might suggest in increased output, as its optional (at no extra cost) Johnson Matthey-supplied dual-loop catalytic converters in link pipes between the manifolds and oval centre box in the dual exhaust (similar to the previous single-side system in the 1986 to 1990 cars) somewhat stifled maximum power and torque. The fuel injection control system had the usual lambda oxygen sensor, non-evaporative fuel lines were used, and (oddly) fuel tank capacity was reduced from 13.4 to 12 gallons. The first of these catalytic converter-fitted Plus 8s was exported to Germany in 1989.

Curiously enough, as implied above, it was possible then to order the car without catalytic converters, in which case power went up a little to 193bhp (DIN), but as the reduction in exhaust obstruction might lead one to expect, at the noticeably increased engine speed of 5,250rpm. The exhaust system in these models was a dual-pipe arrangement with cast iron exhaust manifolds, a single balance pipe between, the exit pipes passing through apertures in the chassis members to a long oval-section front silencer and two round-section resonator boxes. Tyres were as on the standard 3.5 Plus 8, Pirelli P600 205VR-15in.

Lever-arm dampers are banished

In March 1991 Gabriel telescopic dampers were introduced for the rear axle, working from a tubular hoop bolted through the chassis side-members over the axle, at last replacing the ancient lever-arm dampers previously used. Such gas-filled dampers had in fact been used on American export cars for some time previously. It was notable that the added steel hoop needed for these dampers in fact helped to reduce some of the chassis flexibility. Number-plate lighting was now done with two Lucas chromium lights, one each side of the plate, and a smaller reversing lamp was provided.

What *Autocar* & *Motor* thought of the 4 litre

A six-page Test Extra of the 3.9-litre Plus 8 in catalytic converter form was published by *Autocar & Motor* in its 15 May 1991 issue. This report was somewhat patronising in its early part, talking of 'continuous manufacture... of a pre-war car by vintage methods in a vintage factory'. However, it went on to mention the 'six year waiting list' in the order book and was enthusiastic about how it was 'that same vintage character that provides the appeal; drive a Morgan on a sunny day with the roof down, and you've found the antidote to stressful modern living.'

The test became a little more specific about the pleasures of Plus 8 driving, albeit with some hyperbole still. 'The latest 190bhp engine is no more powerful than its predecessor, as a result of those power-sapping catalytic converters, although it does lug with more gusto. Torque is up 7 per cent to 235lb ft at a much lower peak of 2,600rpm. Real stump-wrenching stuff, this.... Plant your right boot hard down on the roller-type throttle pedal until it meets the floorboard – yes, it really is wood – and no matter what gear it happens to be in, the Morgan gathers itself up and launches itself at the horizon with an explosive surge of seemingly unstoppable torque.

'Porsche 911 Turbo drivers, eat your hearts out: for in-gear grunt at normal speeds (in other words, less than 80mph), you won't catch the Morgan. Examine the respective 30–70mph acceleration times in third, fourth and top [fifth] gears for these opposite ends of the sports car spectrum, and the message comes across loud and clear. The 911 Turbo does it [30–70mph] in 7.5, 13.0 and 19.7secs respectively. For Morgan, read 6.0, 8.4 and 12.1secs.'

The car came in for the usual criticism of its ride and deportment over less smooth surfaces, mitigated, however, by the pleasures of driving the Plus 8. 'There are specific types of road to which the Morgan feels perfectly suited. Equally, there are others on which it seems hopelessly inadequate. Its intentionally flexible ladder frame chassis and ash framework, together with short-travel suspension and an axle located by nothing more than a pair of leaf springs, might seem a perverse combination to an engineer in this age of stiff monocoques and precisely controlled all-independent suspension. In theory, the Morgan should handle as though it's hinged in the middle and should rattle like a box of assorted nails, in spite of changes to soften spring rates and improve damping.

'In truth, the Morgan feels tightly assembled even after a high mileage (the test car's odometer was way beyond 18,000 miles), but it only feels truly at home on well-surfaced, winding A and B-roads.... Here, the Plus 8's suspension isn't taxed beyond its limits and the considerable grip of the Avon Turbospeed tyres can be exploited.'

What the 4-litre cost in 1991

	Basic	Tax	Total in UK
Plus 8	£17,950.00	£4,898.85	£22,848.85
Extras			
Leather upholstery	£600.00	£163.75	£763.75
Exterior door handles	£45.00	£12.28	£57.28
Alloy body and wings	£425.00	£115.99	£540.99
Mohair hood	£650.00	£177.40	£827.40
Walnut-veneered facia	£150.00	£40.94	£190.94
Metallic paint	£200.00	£54.58	£254.58
Head restraints	£100.00	£27.29	£127.29

The car's cornering and handling brought mixed if mostly positive views. 'Swing it into a bend and the steering weights up challengingly as you fight against the understeer. Boot the tail out of line on the exit with a whiff of throttle – it seems quite natural with the Morgan – and again you have to wrestle with the low-geared steering to keep it on the island.' This car was built, of course, after the August 1986 change from worm and nut to rack and pinion steering, which was lower geared at 3.5 turns within a not very tight minimum turning circle. The test continued: 'And all the time, you feel everything that's happening through the seat of the pants. This isn't a car for wimps. Total involvement is the message here, sheer exuberance the key to its charm.'

That said, the *Autocar & Motor* testers were critical of the ride over poor roads. 'Bumpy back roads' are 'where the shortcomings in the suspension make themselves ever-present. Damping control is poor, particularly at the rear, suspension travel is inadequate and the rear axle hops and leaps across the road at the least provocation; occasionally, it even bottoms out completely. Morgan's idea of a progressive bumpstop is when the propshaft comes into contact with the top of the propshaft tunnel.'

Nevertheless, for this Road Test team, the Plus 8's charm overcame such complaints. The test ended: 'Yet for some, this intimate involvement of man and

machine against all the odds is the very essence of why the Morgan remains such a dream machine.... The Morgan may be a relic of a bygone era – it could even be thought of as an irrelevance in the '90s – but so long as it continues to create the excitement and challenge epitomised by a tidily driven Plus 8, progress can wait as far as a certain red-brick factory in Malvern is concerned.'

Above: This 4-litre Plus 8 appeared in a 1990s Morgan sales brochure.

A new chassis and other changes

In 1992, Rubery Owen having closed its chassis manufacturing in the late 1970s, Rockwell Thompson bought the Morgan tooling and carried on producing its chassis. However, there was a disagreement between Morgan and Rockwell Thompson about the price being charged, which ended up with the company refusing to renew the contract with Morgan after the Malvern company demanded a substantial price reduction. As a result, production was moved to a local Worcestershire specialist, ABT in Ross-on-Wye. Having built jigs, ABT turned out a dimensionally much more accurate job.

By this time, Europe, including Britain, had adopted stricter exhaust emissions limits, so there was no market for non-catalytic-converter engines and that model disappeared. Also in 1992 or so, customers could specify either rack and pinion or recirculating ball steering. From that year until 1997, there were few changes to the car, apart from detail matters: in early 1993 wire wheels were offered as a option for the first time, and later that summer the original Girling brakes were replaced by servo-assisted Lockheed ones.

Left: In 1993 wire wheels were offered as an option.

Left: Morgan built this unique Plus 8 with a more integrated headlamp treatment.

79

Right: In 1993 the Rover R380 gearbox brought better gear selection, plus safer first and reverse positions. Gear-change quality was improved further by the later RT80 gearbox.

Far right: This 1999 4.6-litre is fitted with Morgan's centre-lock alloy wheels with a 7in rim width.

Below: One side of the powerhouse of the Plus 8 4.6.

New gearbox, bigger engine

In 1993 the then-new Rover R380 gearbox introduced for the new Range Rover became available on the Plus 8. This, besides greater strength and quieter running, endowed it with safer relative positions of first and reverse gears, so that wrong-slotting was far less likely, and also noticeably improved gearchange quality. In 1994 the option of a recirculating ball steering box was dropped, the specification reverting to the more inherently accurate and responsive rack and pinion only, far more appropriate for a true sports car like the Plus 8.

A change in 1994 saw Rover supplying its engines with pumps for power-assisted steering and air conditioning, both surplus to Morgan's requirements. However, the problem was that the drive belt arrangement changed, so Morgan

developed a new drive-belt system, which reversed the rotation of the water pump and, more usefully, involved changing the alternator's location in the process. This modification greatly improved access to the alternator, to the extent that it significantly reduced the time taken to get at the alternator when, for example, needing to replace it. Also, the Rover uprated RT80 gearbox was introduced, giving a further improvement in gearchange. In 1996, one could order a Plus 8 with either 6½in or 7in wide rims, depending on the tyre size selected.

However, in 1997, with the coming of the enlarged engine size to the Rover, it became possible to buy a Plus 8 with the enlarged crankshaft stroke of 82mm instead of 71mm, which took the swept

Left: Underbonnet badge denoting the engine capacity.

Below: Long low shape of a 1999 4.6-litre model with the enlarged cockpit.

Opposite: Cockpit of 1999 4.6-litre displaying better side-locating seats. This car has the larger cockpit but is not fitted with airbags.

Above: A dual-pipe stainless steel exhaust system was fitted in 1997.

Right: Longer doors were a feature of Plus 8s from 1997 onwards.

volume up to 4,552cc. With the same 9.35 compression ratio, this raised the power output by 16 per cent to 220bhp (DIN) at 5,000rpm and the torque by 18.4 per cent to 260lb ft at 3,600rpm instead of 4,750rpm. The only big behind-the-scenes difference was that because the 4.6-litre engine was only available from Rover married to an automatic transmission, it was necessary for Morgan to obtain

the engine from the Rover subsidiary, Powertrain Projects Engineering based in Hinckley. Powertrain produced a special version of the engine for the Malvern company to suit the usual manual transmission. It was special in that the standard version's ECU (engine control unit) was too bulky to be accommodated under the Plus 8's bonnet, so Lucas CUX distributor ignition was fitted instead.

You could still buy the 3.9-litre version and both cars were fitted with higher-geared final drives, at 3.23:1. Maximum speed rose to 128mph, against 124 for the 3.9, and the 0–60mph time was given as 5.6sec. According to Mark Aston, both the 3.9- and 4.6-litre engines had problems with their crankshaft balancing, so that the minor remedial change necessary was to balance the entire drivetrain.

Left: Close-up of instrument panel, showing off the walnut veneer dashboard and part of newly lockable glove compartment lid.

Body changes in 1997

To comply with stricter drive-by noise regulations in 1997, a new stainless steel dual-pipe exhaust system was fitted. Around the same time, GKN-Salisbury-supplied rear axles were replaced with Australian BTR ones, which was a quality improvement, as unlike the Salisbury final drives, the BTR ones never suffered from noise complaints.

A modern dust-free paint shop, introduced that year after delays over the filtration system needed, provided a higher quality paint finish on all Morgan cars, including the Plus 8, and the cockpit underwent the modifications needed to install optional air bags for both front seat occupants. To allow the air bags to operate in an emergency, the dashboard looked as if made from walnut (as before), although in fact it was now formed from a folding aluminium alloy panel covered in a thin walnut veneer. These modifications

were quite considerable and so, in the interests of all the Morgan range and for rationalisation of production, were adopted for all the firm's cars, regardless of whether or not they were airbag-fitted, from mid 1997.

Doors were lengthened rearwards by 2¾in, the heelboard was relocated, as was the dashboard, moved by 2in, and there was a new dished steering wheel to carry the air bag itself. The unseen reasons for this long-overdue enlargement of the cockpit within an unchanged wheelbase included redesigning the rear of the car slightly and the more compact fitting of the battery and fuel system. The overall reason for these modifications was to move the driver back to gain the necessary

clearance distance for the occupant of the driving seat. As is now well known, sitting too close to an inflating air bag is highly counter-productive in terms of occupant protection.

The changes did benefit the car anyway, since as part of this, the seat rails were moved rearwards, providing extra driver legroom and making life better for taller drivers. Another passive safety measure was the fitting of a brace inside the cockpit to improve side-impact protection and body rigidity. It was now possible to adjust the rake of the steering wheel somewhat, if not by as much as is usual with such arrangements. A practical minor detail was the fitting of an enlarged glovebox. These changes were part of the updating and improvement of the Plus 8, which helped it once again to be exported to North America. Exports there had had to stop the year before.

Above: A 1999 4.6-litre showing the bigger cockpit and twin stainless steel exhausts.

Left: Beneath the traditional louvred bonnet lurks the Plus 8's most powerful 4.6-litre V8.

Left: This car is fitted with the four-spoke steering wheel containing an airbag, while the passenger airbag replaces the glovebox.

What *Autocar's* testers thought of the 4.6-litre

Autocar's Road Test of the 4.6 model in the 24 September 1997 issue, noted all the Plus 8 improvements with measured approval, finding the car better than before if still far from perfect by the standards of the day. The car was summed up in the test's introduction: 'If Morgan has done its sums correctly, this promises to be the finest incarnation yet of one of motoring's strangest and most pleasurable phenomenons.'

The article continued: 'Part of the appeal of the Plus 8 is its knack of performing far better than its antiquated looks suggest. Now, with more power than ever before under its louvred bonnet, it has the ability to surprise even a few of today's front-line supercars. The statistic that will wow any bar room bore is that between 50 and 70mph in top, the Morgan is quicker than the Ferrari 550 Maranello, the Porsche 911 GT1, and the TVR Cerbera, covering this benchmark flexibility test in just 5.5sec. Of course, all of these cars are handicapped by taller gearing than the Plus 8 and would demolish the Morgan in a sprint through the gears, but it does give

Below: Autocar's 1997 Road Test car in action, showing how the Plus 8's finely proportioned lines were preserved.

some idea of the effortless way in which the Morgan gathers speed.'

However, performance was hampered by both the engine's limited top-end yield and the chassis. 'The only time the engine fails to deliver is at the top of its rev range. Above 5000rpm, it is disappointingly flat compared with the harder-hitting TVR versions. This and the appalling axle tramp

Left: The large steering wheel and slow, heavy steering were disliked by the Autocar testers.

Far left: The floor-hinged pedals.

Below: Plus 8 4.6-litre test car cornering and described as promising 'to be the finest incarnation yet of one of motoring's strangest yet most pleasurable phenomenons'[sic].

under full-bore standing starts prevent the Plus 8 from reaching 60mph quicker than six seconds dead.'

There were mixed reactions to some of the basic controls. 'The five-speed gearbox has the same chunky feel as all Rover V8 manuals, but the straight, short lever gives it a cleaner throw than the previous angled item. The floor-mounted brake pedal [they meant floor-hinged] by contrast, is heavy, prone to lock-up and difficult to modulate, hence the poor 60–0mph time of 4.1sec.'

Also the handling did not meet contemporary standards, according to the *Autocar* Road Test team. 'Part of the problem is the steering, which manages to combine the two faults of being both excessively heavy and worryingly slow (3.0 turns between locks), with a vastly oversized steering wheel to control it. As a result, you end up steering from the shoulders, leaning into the corners and bracing your weight against the wheel, feeling for all the world like a Bentley Boy on a qualifying lap at Brooklands.

'This is all very well until the power finally overwhelms the grip of the 205/55ZR16 Pirellis and the back steps out. You then have fractions of a second to unwind the steering, apply the corrective lock and slingshot out of the corner in a perfectly controlled power slide. Get it right, and you will be congratulating yourself for years to come; get it wrong and you will be sweeping up wood splinters from the gutter.

'Of course, any other lightweight special like a Caterham 7 or Lotus Elise would have long disappeared without so much as a wobble. We can't help feeling that a Morgan that handled more predictably would be no less desirable because of it, even if the driving experience wasn't quite as evocative.'

For all its obvious failings, the Morgan Plus 8 if anything succeeds in earning higher praise and enthusiasm from this *Autocar* Road Test than ever before. The article ends as usual with *Autocar*'s verdict on the car. 'However much you want to slam the Morgan for its outdated dynamics and chronic ergonomics, it is hard not to be won over by the skill of the craftsmanship and the undiluted character of the driving experience. You are not merely buying a car, but a perfectly preserved piece of motoring history. We cannot imagine people seriously trying to decide between a Morgan and a TVR. They are two completely different machines designed to fulfil two totally different requirements...

'Therefore, it seems fruitless to judge the Morgan by objective criteria alone.

That's not to say that the Plus 8 is unable to compete on a facts and figures basis – it is extremely rapid by most standards, and below most people's expectations of pricing – but there is a whole lot more to owning a Morgan than the usual list of pros and cons. For the full experience, you need to go to the factory itself and watch each ash wood frame being carefully cut, shaped and glued into place before having the hand-beaten aluminium bodywork made to measure.

'Nor is it fair to describe the end result as an irrelevant anachronism. Morgan is not averse to change, so long as it does not affect the overall character of the car. The latest improvements have made it safer, more comfortable to live with and able to meet all the latest noise and emissions regulations. We have no doubt that it could also have engineered such comparatively simple items as power steering, assisted brakes and independent coil-sprung rear suspension. The point is that it chose not to for fear of veering too far from the Morgan experience.

'Whether you agree with that standpoint is another matter. We don't. But until that fabled six-year waiting list starts to drop, there seems little point in arguing with the masters of survival.'

Below: One of the best angles from which to view the Plus 8.

Left: Plus 8 body may have been old-fashioned in 1997 but is undeniably most handsome.

Below: The 1997 4.6-litre Autocar test car at speed with optional mohair hood, which 'looks far better than standard PVC item'.

Above: The visitor's approach to the Morgan factory's reception area and showroom.

Building a Plus 8

Production of Morgans at the Malvern Link factory was a fascinating process, since although featuring many modern treatments and techniques, it was fundamentally of a much earlier period and gained the benefit of a great deal of individual craftsman work.

Right: Plus 8 MMC 11 (in its second manifestation) on display in the Morgan factory's showroom.

The visitor's introduction to the factory is via reception on the right-hand side of the entrance road from Gate B down into the plant. The walls of this room are hung with historic panels and photographs and even portraits, notably of the firm's founder, H. F. S. Morgan.

Chassis frames, built for Morgan by ABT in Ross-on-Wye, consisted of Z-section longitudinals linked by same-section cross-members placed at strategic areas, such as just behind and under the front of the transmission casing, in the front end of the car, and each end of the rear leaf springs. The springs pivoted from the forward end within the longitudinals and were connected by shackles at the rear end. The zinc-coating introduced was done the proper way, not by pre-coated steel but after frame assembly, by dipping in a tank of molten zinc – similar to the method used by Porsche to this day. Lesser parts, such as brackets, valances, and even hood frames, were either galvanised or, using a facility in the Morgan plant, powder-coated. When the completed chassis arrived at Malvern, it was drilled to provide fixing locations for components like the suspension, engine and gearbox mounts and so on. Before assembly of the suspension to the chassis, the wooden floorboards in treated marine plywood were put into place. Another sheet of wood was used to provide a supporting floor for the fuel tank, which itself was made within the plant and not provided by any outside supplier.

An obvious material, high in terms of quantity, on the supply list was ash for the frame of the body. This type of hardwood had a number of advantages over other sorts of timber. Its strength to weight ratio was, by the already high standards of wood, amongst the highest, to the notable extent that it was used to support the anchorages for the seat belts, while its splinter-resistant nature was a modern attribute in terms of crash safety never dreamt of when it was first introduced for Morgan bodies way back. Around five tons of ash, mainly from British sources, was used each year. The wood was kiln-dried before being stored for a year or so of seasoning in the firm's timber collection.

Largest component of the body in ash was the rear wheelarches, made with laminated ash, formed into the necessary curved shapes by clamping under heat in

a special chamber. Each frame was put together by an individual craftsman, using joints specially cut, glued, and screwed together. When complete the frame was dipped in a bath of Cuprinol preservative before being hung up to dry. Fixing to the chassis frame was done with zinc-coated steel coach bolts, with a waterproof membrane between the wood and the steel.

The body panels were never something provided from the press shop of an outside

Far left: A rolling chassis with ash frame for the body in the factory yard in 1992.

Left: Morgan hung this chassis on the wall of its stand at the 1998 British Motor Show at the NEC, Birmingham.

Below: Ash body frames in the woodshop at the Morgan factory.

Right: A craftsman works on the ash body frame.

Right: Plus 8s (on left) in the factory bodyshop in 1994.

Right: A skilled panel-beater at work.

Far right: The classic radiator grille is made in the sheet-metal shop

firm but were formed in the sheet metal shop at Malvern in the traditional way by craftsmen using hammers, mallets, rolling wheels, hand presses etc. – all the tools of a skilled panel-beater. Each car had its panels individually formed to fit it – there was no attempt made to achieve needless production uniformity, so that in the event of any crash damage, the car required replacement bodywork made to suit that particular vehicle, something the adaptability of the Morgan method made entirely feasible. The Plus 8's wings with their wired edges were the only exception, being made and supplied from outside. Nevertheless, it was remarkable how much of the car was made at the factory – another example was the radiator grille, an assembly of carefully arranged bars done in the sheet-metal shop.

Assembly started with the placing of the chassis on to trestles at a convenient height for working and the engine-gearbox unit being lowered on to the chassis using a hand-operated hoist. Then followed the fitting of the steel front wheel valances used to support the wings, the front bulkhead, the suspension, steering, brakes and their supply lines. Assembly of suspension parts into ready-to-fit units had been done by the machine shop.

In the old paint shop (used before the completion of the new one housing the water-based spray system), the cars went through masked up and on slave wheels to avoid overspray in the wrong places. The bonnets and bolted-on wings were left off to ensure good painting around and under the joints. Cleaning to remove dirt and so on from the body was then followed by sanding by hand, after epoxy filler had been used to deal with any production blemishes. Five coats of a matt primer were applied before final sanding and the spraying of the top coat. The finished body was then reunited with its wings with colour-beading fitted at the joints to finish them off tidily while adding an extra barrier to rust formation. The bonnet was left off for ease of assembly of engine accessories and so on. Wiring looms were added at this stage, as were the exhaust system and catalytic converter, and lamps.

We noted earlier that a remarkable proportion of the parts for the Plus 8 were made or machined by the Malvern Link factory. The list of the machine shop's produce was impressive: hood frames, shackle pins, steering dampers, brake drums, discs, hubs, stub axles, front suspension, engine mounts, and bonnet catches, to name but a few.

Above: A Plus 8 in the wiring shop in 1994.

Left: Machine shop at Morgan's Malvern Link factory.

The trim shop, mostly staffed by women, was where the addition of seats, carpets, upholstery, badges, hood and so on happened. Standard trim material was black PVC, with Connolly leather optional, although requested by many customers. Four hides were required for the Plus 8.

After final assembly, wing undersides were black-waxed, whilst in the subsequent dispatch shop, bumpers were fitted and the car was checked for any final touching up and so on. Then followed a road test, a final feature undergone by every Morgan. Including the smaller-engined Plus 4s, the factory then turned out around two cars every day.

Far left and left: Badges were fitted in the trim shop.

Far left: Upholsterers at work.

Left: A completed Plus 8 waits outside the trim shop in 1994.

Left: A completed Plus 8 (minus its radiator grille) ready for its road test in 1998.

Right: A Plus 8 fitted with Morgan's centre-lock light alloy wheels.

Far right: Morgan's centre-lock 7J 16in light alloy wheel specially made for the firm.

Below: The Plus 8 Anniversary model.

Final days of the Plus 8

The Plus 8 continued in production at Malvern up to 2004, three years into the production of its modern successor, the Aero 8, which is detailed in the following chapters. Nothing of great note happened to the Plus 8 between 1999 and 2002 when the 4.6-litre V8 was dropped, leaving only the 3.9-litre version powering the now 35-year-old Morgan. Power output was then quoted as 190bhp at 4,850rpm (maximum power had been stated as occurring at 100rpm lower engine speed), whilst peak torque was slightly reduced, from 235lb ft to 225lb ft at 2,600rpm.

The Plus 8 disappeared from the Morgan range in May 2004, when the last Plus 8 was seen, basically because MG Rover's new owner, BMW, declared that it intended to stop production of the V8 engine. This was chiefly because it was felt that the work necessary get the engine through the Euro III emissions level was not worthwhile, particularly as BMW planned to put its own engines in the larger MG Rover vehicles.

The Roadster V6

However, the chassis and body lived on, appearing as they did in a smaller-engined version called the Morgan Roadster V6 in the summer of 2004. This was powered by a Ford V6 engine, an 89.0mm x 79.5mm bore and stroke 2,967cc four-valves-per-cylinder unit. With a 10:1 compression ratio, this engine produced 223bhp at 6,150rpm and 210lb ft of torque at 4,900rpm, giving the car a 0–60mph time of 4.9sec and a maximum speed of 134mph. It worked through a five-speed gearbox, with gear ratios of: first 4.23:1, second 2.52:1, third 1.67:1, fourth 1.22:1, and top 1.00:1. There was a choice of three different final drives (3.45:1, 3.23:1, and 3.08:1), all fitted with a 30 per cent limited slip differential. This was altogether a tolerably performing substitute for the various V8s of the true Plus 8, if somewhat higher revving.

As those performance figures suggest,

Left: The 3-litre Ford V6 engine installed in a Roadster chassis.

Left: Partly completed Roadster rolling chassis. Note the aluminium wings stacked behind.

Morgan Plus 8 and its rivals in 1997

Make and Model	Top speed	0–60mph	0–100mph ¼-mile	Standing consumption	Fuel inc tax	Price
Alfa Romeo 2.0 Spider	122mph	9.4sec	29.2sec	17.3sec	29mpg	£23,034
BMW Z3 2.8	134mph	6.7sec	18.4sec	15.2sec	27mph	£28,115
Caterham 21 Supersport	127mph	6,7sec	18.7sec	15.8sec	33mpg	£25,495
Jaguar XK8 4.0	155mph	6.6sec	16.7sec	15.2sec	22mpg	£57,300
Lotus Elise 1.8i	124mph	5.5sec	17.4sec	14.4sec	33mpg	£20,950
Mazda MX5 1.8i	115mph	10.1sec	32.1sec	17.6sec	28mpg	£15,410
MGF 1.8i	123mph	8.7sec	27.0sec	16.6sec	30mpg	£17,440
Morgan Plus 8 4.6	128mph	6.0sec	15.3sec	14.5sec	21mpg	£32,489
Porsche Boxter 2.5	139mph	6.5sec	18.0sec	15.6sec	29mpg	£33,950
TVR Chimaera 4.0	158mph	5.2sec	13.2sec	13.8sec	26mpg	£30,650
Westfield 3.9 SEiGHT	140mph	4.3sec	10.5sec	13.2sec	–	£25,950

Opposite: The Roadster in its more usual open guise.

Right: Morgan Roadster V6, the last gasp of the Plus 8, which inherited its mantle on the Plus 8's demise in 2004. This example is fitted with a hardtop.

Centre: Cockpit of the Roadster closely recalls its Plus 8 heritage, as do the controls.

Below: Interior of the four-seater Roadster offered proper accommodation for four adults. This car has the optional extra natural wood dashboard and centre console, and elasticated door pockets. The wood-rimmed Moto Lita steering wheel was an aftermarket fitment.

Below right: The four-seater Roadster had a completely new hood and spare wheel mounting. This car has the optional extra stainless steel wire wheels.

his undeniable standing as a very distinguished and advanced modern automotive engineer, as quoted in the next chapter. The Roadster achieved this with its relative lightness (its kerb weight was 2,072lb) combined with power and torque figures not too far short of the Plus 8's V8 in its last form.

That balance of form echoed one of the Roadster features often mentioned by road tests of the period – its near ideal weight distribution. Despite the construction of the Ford engine's cylinder block – cast iron where the original Rover V8's block was aluminium alloy – the unit was not too heavy, whilst its compactness allowed it to be mounted comparatively well back behind the radiator. The car was also the beneficiary of the latest in what development the Plus 8 had undergone, most obviously in the shape of its rack and pinion steering in place of the original worm and nut system. Wheels were bolt-on aluminium alloy five-stud 6.5 x 15in shod with 205/55 tyres, with the option of wider section stainless-steel 72-spoke 7 x 16in wire wheels carrying the same section tyres. In 2006 the Roadster was also available as a four-seater version, the back seats folding down to form a luggage platform when not required. The Roadster four-seater then cost £33,300 plus £5,827.50 UK tax, making a total of £39,127.50 for home market purchasers.

the Roadster V6 was a good, reasonably acceptable replacement for the Plus 8, sustaining Morgan's undeniable appeal to those traditional-minded enthusiast customers for whom the Aero 8's undeniable advances in up-to-date chassis and suspension design were irrelevant. It did so not least, of course, by its faithful retention of the visually perfect balance of its historic lines so much admired by Jim Randle, notwithstanding

Right: Morgan Roadster's Ford 3-litre V6.

Tougher emissions regulations

How did Morgan manage at this time in meeting the now steeper requirements of exhaust emission regulations? It is obvious that passive safety was something that the chassis designers – Morgan themselves – had to do but, given that engines were supplied from outside the company, was not the engine manufacturer to be relied upon to provide a power unit which met the emissions rules? The author put this point to Mark

Aston and was most interested in his reply.

'No – originally you could to a certain extent but with the levels of emissions you are talking about in the last ten years, it is independent of the engine maker – changing the mass of the vehicle is enough to make a difference. On-board diagnostics is one of the most difficult things to deal with, because the effects of loads on the engine and the characteristics change the sensing of the on-board diagnostics,

putting the 'mil' light on in some cars, so it is more tricky sometimes than getting the emissions right.

'So, yes, you are looking for an engine with the right emissions but you are also looking for the back-up. Where Ford came out really well, why we went the route with the V6, was that they were able to offer the support and back-up to tune the ECUs and to modify them – because all ECUs on the Morgan are latterly a unique specification. You got through the 1980s using the original specification, but in the 1990s we found that when we were doing that, we were running into problems. The 4-4 1800 with the Ford Zetec engine in was OK, and it went quite well, and it wasn't a bad little engine. Fuel consumption was great but driving characteristics were not perfect, because you were reliant on the Ford tune, with a few little tweaks, and that never worked. With the new Roadster version of the Plus 8 with the V6 Ford engine, we went for a complete tune to our own specification, based around the Ford one obviously, but we did get the driving characteristics right.'

What the Roadster 3-litre V6 cost in 2008

	Basic	Tax	Total in UK
Roadster 2-seater	£31,850.00	£5,573.75	£37,423.75
Roadster 4-seater	£34,465.00	£6,031.38	£40,496.38
Extras			
16in stainless steel wire wheels	£1,900.00	£332.50	£2,232.50
Air conditioning	£1,525.00	£266.88	£1,791.88
Dashboard body colour (2-seater)	£300.00	£52.50	£352.50
Walnut dashboard (2-seater), plus leather centre console (4-seater)	£325.00	£56.88	£381.88
Natural wood dashboard and centre console (4-seater)	£700.00	£122.50	£822.50
Leather upholstery (2-seater)	£1,250.00	£218.75	£1,468.75
Leather upholstery (4-seater)	£1,605.00	£280.88	£1,885.88
Full-width bumpers (2-seater)	£375.00	£65.63	£440.63

Specifications: 1991 Morgan Plus 8 (4-litre)

ENGINE

Description
Overhead valve push-rod V8 with aluminium alloy block and pressed in 'dry' cast iron liners, aluminium alloy cross-flow cylinder head. Chain-driven single camshaft in the vee operating two valves per cylinder via short pushrods and hydraulic tappets. Three-ring aluminium alloy pistons, steel connecting rods, and shell bearings. Five-bearing cast iron crankshaft with torsional vibration damper. Two catalytic converters. Electric cooling fan

Capacity
3,946cc (240.8cu in)

Bore and stroke
94.0mm x 71.12mm (3.70in x 2.80in)

Compression ratio
9.35:1

Maximum power
190bhp (DIN) (141kW) @ 4,750rpm

Maximum torque
230lb ft (312Nm) @ 2,600rpm

Fuelling
Lucas/Bosch LE fuel injection

TRANSMISSION

Gearbox
Rover five speed all synchromesh

Ratios

1st	3.32:1
2nd	2.08:1
3rd	1.39:1
4th	1.00:1
Top	0.79:1
Reverse	3.42:1

Clutch
Borg and Beck, 9½in single dry plate

Propshaft
Hardy Spicer, needle roller bearings

Rear axle
Salisbury hypoid bevel, ratio 3.31:1. Powr-Lok limited slip differential

BRAKES

Front
Girling disc, 11.0in

Rear
Girling drum, 9in x 1¾in

Operation
Girling dual circuit hydraulic

Handbrake
Fly-off lever with cable linkage to rear drums

SUSPENSION

Front
Independent. Sliding pillars, coil springs, telescopic dampers

Rear
Half-elliptic springs with live rear axle, Gabriel telescopic dampers

STEERING

System type
Jack Knight rack and pinion or Gemmer recirculating ball, collapsible column

Number of turns lock to lock
3¼ (3½ with 14in wheel)

Turning circle
38ft 0in (11.6m)

Steering wheel
Astrali three-spoke, 15in (optional 14in) diameter

WHEELS AND TYRES
6½J x 15in cast aluminium alloy wheels

Tyres
205/60VR-15in Avon radial ply

PERFORMANCE
Autocar & Motor Test Extra, 15 May 1991

Top speed

121mph (195kph)	
0–50mph (80kph)	4.7sec
0–60mph (96kph)	6.1sec
0–70mph (112kph)	8.5sec
0–80mph (128kph)	10.6sec
0–90mph (144kph)	13.7sec
0–100mph (160kph)	18.4sec
0–110mph (177kph)	23.6sec
Standing quarter mile (402m)	15.1sec

Overall fuel consumption
20.1mpg (14.1l/100km)

DIMENSIONS

Length
13ft 0in (3,962mm)

Width
5ft 3in (1,600mm)

Height (hood up)
4ft 4in (1,321mm)

Wheelbase
8ft 2in (2,438mm)

Track
Front: 4ft 5in (1,346m)
Rear: 4ft 6in (1,372mm)

Ground clearance
5½in (140mm)

Weight
2,059lb (934kg)

Design, development and production

Four years or so before the 1999 beginning of the Plus 8's fourth (and final) part-decade, Morgan's management was starting to wonder about the future of the company, particularly after the dawn of the new millennium. Did the firm not need some sort of radically more modern car? This would not necessarily depart too far from the Morgan formula of building sports car bodies in an old style, which the company had followed so very successfully in the postwar era. Nevertheless something new could be a very good idea – amid the potentially contentious question of what exactly ought to be new and what of the traditional Morgan to preserve – that would ensure the company's future into the new millennium. All credit too to this relatively ancient family firm, based on traditional methods of manufacture, for looking so carefully at techniques hugely in advance of the way it had successfully done things so far, and for so long, to the satisfaction of so many Morgan customers.

The BMW connection

Charles Morgan tells the story of the time of the Plus 8's end and the Roadster very entertainingly. 'I was told the Rover engine finishes by 2005, so we had to find an alternative V8, and I'd approached BMW and the two projects came beautifully together, because what happened was, in 1998, we were motor racing against the McLaren F1. Of course, BMW sponsored the Alpina BMW long tail – fantastic car – and it was quite extraordinary to have this car in the same race as a Morgan.

'Anyway, we were at Nürburgring and in the next-door pit to McLaren. And the McLaren, needless to say, won the race – first, second, third, Nelson Piquet was one of their drivers – and we came in very near the end but finished this six-hour race. And blow me down, Wolfgang Reitzle and Karl-Heinz Kalbfell came through into our pit after the race and warmly shook us by the hand, saying: "The best thing today is we won the race; the second best thing is that the Morgan finished."

Right: The 1997 Morgan Plus 8 GTR from which the Aero 8 was developed.

'And I said: "Well, we would go a bit quicker if we had one of your engines" – and within two weeks, Karl-Heinz had come to see my father and me. We went up to a hotel in Malvern and did the deal.

'We were the only people with an official contract with BMW to use certain of their petrol engines and have that system for motor sport. But it has always been a good relationship – sadly Karl-Heinz has now joined Fiat and Alfa and Maserati, which is a real pain, but I've kept in with a few of the top people within BMW. But a lot of people have since left – the guy who designed the engine has gone to Ford. But he made the memorable comment on testing the car at Miramas: "At last we have a chassis to show how good my engine is." Which he didn't want repeating when he worked

at BMW. All their cars are too heavy, that was his point.

'Once that was done, we very quickly started to plan a project with BMW. So the two things happened – the motor racing carried on, right up to the end of 1998, then that stopped, and then, 1999 was spent both here and at Munich designing the new car. So the BMW project started probably about the end of 1998. It was a big project for us, big investment; this was a proper project – OK, not a mass volume, but certainly the same sort of project that for example they would put the M5 through. So that meant high speed testing at Miramas, and then hot weather testing, and endless days in the BMW emissions laboratories – and to be honest, that was a very, very big step for us.'

Left: An Aero 8 Series 1 and Peter Morgan's Plus 8 at the factory.

Left: Charles Morgan photographed within the grounds of the Morgan factory.

The honeycomb experiment

Charles Morgan was asked to visit the various racing car manufacturers based in Britain to have a look at the latest technologies for chassis manufacture. Carbon fibre was ruled out for the obvious reason of its exorbitant expense at the time, which put it well beyond the boundaries set by the roadgoing sports car market. What did at first appear more feasible was to adopt honeycomb material, exemplified in the Ciba-Geigy supply to the Jaguar XJ220 project. Professor Woodley at Ciba-Geigy helped Morgan build the tub, which was then taken to Rhoddy Harvey-Bailey and turned into a competition version of a Morgan.

However, it was run on the road initially – in road-legal form of course – then in a tolerably successful competition car but its practicality for a production road car was obviously low. Metallic honeycomb derives its impressive strength-to-weight ratio from being and remaining complete and integrated, in its innate thickness and lightweight walls. This is fine in structures like aeroplane wings where the major load – aerodynamic lift

– is spread over the entire area of each wing. However, in a car chassis frame there are very few of what structural mathematics calls a uniformly distributed load – virtually all loads are applied at concentrated points on the frame or bodyshell. Therefore, applying any load on a honeycomb structure was made difficult by the fact that application and attaching the load such as, say, a suspension pivot or a spring/damper mounting, required that the load must be spread over a wide area. The honeycomb's thin walls meant that brackets were a real challenge to design, make, and apply to the material.

There was also the problem of electrolytic differential corrosion when something non-aluminium like steel had to be attached to the aluminium alloy of the honeycomb. Also, in a road car intended to carry at least a driver and passenger, there was the space lost by the thickness of honeycomb (around 1in), which made this structurally advanced material impractical. Finally, the ultimate failing was its cost, which became obvious when talking to the manufacturers of the XK220, Abbey Panels, which spoke of circa £25,000–£30,000 per chassis. This put honeycomb totally out of court.

Below: The Aero 8 prototype, complete with tape disguise.

Right: Aluminium Aero 8 Series 1 chassis at the factory.

Right: Jim Randle at his Welford-on-Avon home.

Bonded aluminium chassis

Fortunately, just at that time, Charles Morgan encountered Colin Scott of Alcan, manufacturers and suppliers of aluminium alloys, which has a base at Banbury in Oxfordshire. From him Charles learnt of work Alcan was doing with the mainstream production side of Jaguar on a new technique involving the joining of aluminium alloy very effectively by bonding. Morgan was not unfamiliar with bonding through its work with honeycomb material but what Alcan was talking about was much more interesting. It revealed that bonding aluminium alloy could result in a chassis with virtually double the stiffness compared to conventional sheet-joining methods. The simple reason was that in contrast with a bolted, riveted, or spot-welded joint, bonding could unite the entire area of the joining surfaces, analogous to a seam-welded joint but even more effective because, if properly done, it ensured the whole joint was made, not just the edges.

Charles Morgan tells how, although not a professionally trained engineer himself, he discovered how effective the bonding technique could be in miniature by making a paper card replica, glued together, of the proposed new chassis. He says that it was whilst he was engaged in this (in spare moments), he met former Jaguar chief engineer Jim Randle, who was already working on his own variant of a bonding technique for sports car chassis. Jim was now unconnected with Jaguar, but not Alcan and its products, as he had become firmly acquainted with aluminium alloy techniques with Alcan during the spare-time evolution of the Jaguar XJ220. Then Jaguar, later famous for the aluminium alloy bonded and riveted unitary chassis of the XJ8 saloon, was still only looking at the technology and at Alcan.

Randle then helped Morgan by designing, and getting his friend Tim Payne of Park Sheet Metal to build an aluminium alloy bonded and riveted sheet chassis, which would double as a new modern chassis for the Plus 8 and as the chassis for the Aero 8. It was in fact based on a similar chassis Jim had designed with Tim Payne to produce for the proposed revival of Lea-Francis. Jim's old friend and Jaguar associate, the distinguished designer/stylist Keith Helfet, drew and produced a ¼-scale all-enveloping body for

Right and opposite: Keith Helfet's ¼-scale model of the proposed modern Morgan was quite different from the subsequent Aero 8.

the new Morgan. As our photographs show, though modern, this recalled the Morgan heritage in both its front and wing line.

Thanks to this, and given that Jim's own chassis work had been in conjunction with Park Sheet Metal, it was natural that it was this Coventry-based company that was used to build the first chassis, using pre-treated aluminium alloy (to ensure that the bonding had the right surfaces to bond to), and a blind-riveting system. Randle had already been working on and developing his ideas on this system of building an aluminium alloy chassis, which was in fairly advanced shape when he got briefly involved with Morgan. Jim Randle picks up his end of the tale here: 'What happened was, I went along with Keith Helfet and we offered to Charles the prospect of doing a modern Morgan, in which I would do the chassis and the under-structure and Keith would do the styling.

'And we actually produced, at our own cost, a ¼-scale model of the body, which we took along; at the same time I took along the ideas for a structure. I had always worked with Alcan – we worked with Alcan for the Jaguar XJ220, that's how Jaguar got into aluminium cars. The structure I evolved for the Morgan was originally designed to go under the Plus 8 body – in fact, we later crash-tested it under a Morgan Plus 8, when it crashed extremely well – outstanding, in fact. I knew Colin Scott of Alcan very well. And the first car was a tub, which is very similar to the one which went into the Aero 8, but with a space-frame front end – very much like a D-type, in fact an E-type – very similar. But once we'd started work, I soon concluded that I wasn't going to get the crash performance out of that sort of structure.'

In spite of the engineering background from his Jaguar time being very different from the way Morgan did things, Jim was very impressed with the looks of the Plus 8 and with many of the Morgan Motor Co's people at that time. He particularly admired Peter Morgan: 'I thought Peter Morgan was a super guy and he had some very good ideas, and business management ideas too. I remember him saying: "Yes, that's fine, I like what you're doing, but don't let it cost more than £40,000," and

Right: Peter Morgan, pictured in his office, impressed Jim Randle.

Below: Jim Randle is an admirer of the Plus 8's style and balance.

Suspension design

At some juncture during this co-operation, Chris Lawrence, formerly a very successful competition Morgan driver, but also an experienced mechanic with a particular interest in suspension, appeared on the Morgan scene to join the company, eventually becoming its director of engineering. Although Jim Randle had some interesting and original ideas of how to suspend the proposed new car, they were still in the process of negotiation for a patent, so they could not be used immediately; meanwhile, Lawrence had his own ideas.

It was the Lawrence cum Harvey-Bailey suspension that Morgan favoured on account of its well-known design along established lines. Charles Morgan had doubts about the production viability of Jim Randle's ingenious ideas, so for the moment the work on the new proposal in competition car form first was divided into Chris Lawrence doing the suspension and, says Charles, Jim Randle with Charles Morgan working on the chassis structure.

'I also liked Chris Lawrence,' explained Jim Randle, 'we managed to discuss ideas

very well. But eventually I decided I'd rather be out of it and I sold Charles the chassis, as it was to that stage. He wanted to put a different front end on to suit the front suspension work that they had done, which I didn't particularly like, and I said: "Well, OK, I'll do the chassis up to the bulkhead and you can put your front end on if you like." And really that is about where it was and I sold him the rights to build that chassis for Morgans – but only for Morgans.

'In its original form, the complete chassis including my own front cross-member, had a good torsional stiffness, of around 6,000Nm/degree, and also returned an extremely good crash test result, helped by that cross-member. This, however, was removed latterly by Morgan who substituted their own front cross-member which was designed for the Harvey-Bailey front suspension, which being originally designed for racecar use, had very long wishbones to reduce camber change.'

That arrangement is fine for a racing car application, where there is very little suspension movement, but less helpful

he was absolutely right. That's where Morgan's market really was, just to sort of supplement the Plus 8 as it was at the time. Frankly, looking at the Plus 8, I think the Plus 8 style, and I still think so, has a balance that is exactly right – all of it, the skin, form, shape – it gives you an idea of what's going on beneath the skin. I think that is a lovely little car.'

in a road car, where some suspension movement is desirable, even on a sports car. There is therefore roll, for which shorter unequal-length wishbones can be arranged to compensate. The car's Harvey-Bailey front suspension further borrowed from racing car practice by adopting single-seater cantilever springing, used to get the spring/damper unit out of the slipstream and avoid unnecessary extra aerodynamic drag. So the spring/damper is moved inside the body and worked by extending one wishbone inboard, its inner end operating the unit.

The disadvantage of this on a road car is that the fulcrum about which the wishbone works is subject to highly magnified loads, which do not allow any road-vibration absorbing flexible pivot bush. In the Morgan case, this problem was ignored – at the expense of road noise – by using a Rose joint (a solid balljoint familiar to racing car designers).

Keith Helfet's Aero 8 design

After Jim Randle and I had finished discussing his time working on the Morgan chassis, Jim led me over to Kenilworth to talk to Keith Helfet, who still has the photos and model of his suggestion for the Aero 8 body. On seeing this in Keith's house, I thought that his suggestion had been ideal for the car. While being basically still up-to-date in appearance, and very beautiful, it still carried several strong suggestions of the Morgan line, particularly in its nose and the way that the sides recalled the Plus 8 wing line. Keith was interesting in his discussion of the subject, a brief quotation showing some of his thinking about what was a big challenge.

'It is difficult, and I've had to do it several times, trying to design a kind of successor to an icon – I think that all of these things are trying to do that and it's tough. One has, however, to respect what is there before but, having said that, not to do a pastiche – and that's what most people do, they take a few graphic elements and just put it on whatever – whereas the Plus 8 has some wonderful form, sculpture to it, and I did try to capture some of that.'

Above left: The Aero 8's front suspension.

Above: Rear suspension and ventilated disc brake.

Left: Rear suspension assembly viewed from above.

Below: Jim Randle's designer/stylist colleague Keith Helfet and the ¼-scale model of the Aero 8 body he and Jim proposed.

Chris Lawrence's involvement

Chris Lawrence, who had a strong connection through his own company Lawrencetune with Morgan in its Plus 4 heyday, became involved with the Malvern team again during the gestation of what eventually became the Aero 8. His aspect of those early days is well worth considering:

'I'd worked out I needed to go back to work, so I took myself to Morgan, and Peter and Charles took me out to lunch and I told them that I had a great plan for building a 2-litre out of the Plus 4 that they were building then. It was a detailed plan and they looked at it and the outcome of it was would I go and see if I could do anything with this existing honeycomb car for three months?

'So, I thought, "well, at least I've got my foot in the door" – but, whilst I was there on my second visit, I fell over the steel sheet mock-up of Randle's chassis, which wasn't quite what Morgan needed. For a number of reasons – the doorway was in the wrong place, the detail doesn't matter – it didn't really suit. And it was sitting

there, made out of sheet steel just as a mock-up to demonstrate the design, and I said to Charles straight away: "Now come on, that's what we want. Why can't we make that in aluminium? That's good.

'Charles Morgan explained: "It's a design by Jim Randle and they are making one in aluminium and it's supposed to be bonded with a special Alcan process and riveted, and it's supposed to be very light and it's going to be very rigid."

'And I said: "Well, come on, let's have some, then we'll go racing and then we might get somewhere." Anyway, I went and hacked this previous honeycomb thing to pieces; I sort of bolted it together again and we did the 1996 European GT Championship. We were the slowest car in the field by quite a margin. We got several points, Heaven knows how, and we finished five races out of nine, which took everybody aback completely, because it had never finished before, and they were all four- and six-hour races.

'This was half the honeycomb – I hacked

most of it off and made it work. Wickham drove the wheels off it and Charles Morgan was very good, he can drive like the wind. And we had a good year – I did it at the factory, so there I was, known to Peter, a devil he knew and working in-house. And then the first aluminium tub turned up, from Park Sheet Metal, from Jim. It still wasn't quite right for Morgan, there was absolutely no front end at all and just a square hole in the back, no rear suspension, just the tub. Anyway, I thought about it and I hacked it up and I put a diffuser under the back and opened up the door aperture. I hacked it about 'till it was a Morgan and it would take the Plus 8 body properly.

'I did it over a weekend when there was nobody in there and when they came in on Monday, there it was. So we went from there and I built a front end. Jim was very funny about the front, he said he had designed it, but it was always secret because it had a patented weight transfer system for a cross-member and he wouldn't release it because the patent hadn't gone through. I wanted to build the car and go racing in 1997 with it. Anyway, in the end Morgan bought him out. Then the whole project became Morgan and I got a chap to come and work with me – he was already there. He worked in the machine shop and he could work AutoCAD, and I redesigned it completely differently with a completely new front end and did the rear subframe.'

Chris worked on the new chassis and eventually approached Peter Morgan to get his approval. 'I said: "Look, we've made something special here, worthy of the Morgan name in my opinion. Let me build a prototype and let Charles continue negotiation with BMW, we'll put a Beemer in it if we possibly can, and you are going to have something out of the ordinary." And he said: "Yes, OK, off you go." He was no trouble at all and said: "What's it going to cost ?" I said: "I've no idea, but I'll keep it down."

'That was the sort of understanding we had, so that's how it all started. I worked on it alone for two years and I went with

Below: Chris Lawrence, who became Morgan's chief development engineer.

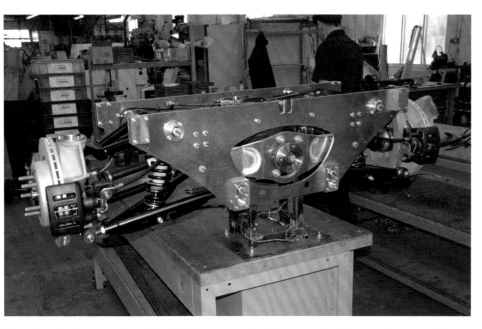

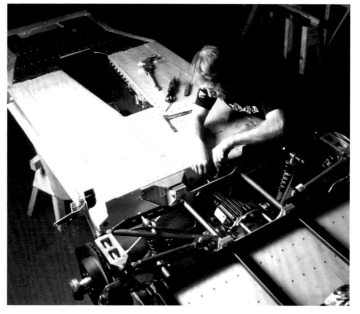

him, but Charles negotiated the BMW, because no one else was getting Beemer engines in those days, nobody. So that was a coup and that goes to Charles, definitely. I went with him, and I did the technical stuff, but he was the charm, the negotiator, no question about it. So we got

the Beemer and, of course, it was a piece of sheer magic to me – this thing was unbelievable – I can sum it up very quickly.

'The last progress meeting I went to, when we'd already made 300 cars, under Any Other Business at the end of the meeting, there was BMW asking, "Can we

have a quick survey of what problems he's had with the engines?" To which there was a stony silence, so eventually I said: "Well, the silence is because we haven't had any." That drew the inevitable question: "What, in 300 engines, you haven't had a single problem?" I said: 'No, not yet.'

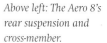

Above left: The Aero 8's rear suspension and cross-member.

Above: The underside of the aluminium alloy chassis, viewed from the rear end.

Far left: Taking the digital measurements used for building the production versions.

Left: A panel-beater at work on a component for an Aero 8 chassis.

The BMW V8 engine

The 4.4-litre BMW V8 was, of course, a most interesting engine. In September 1995 when it first appeared in the BMW 7-series saloon, it was a new member of the M60 family of engines first seen over three years earlier in 3- and 4-litre forms in the revised 7-series at the March 1992 Geneva Show. Compared to the 4-litre, the 4,398cc engine's bore was enlarged by 3mm to 92mm and its stroke by 2.7mm to 82.7mm, so it remained significantly 'over-square', meaning its bore was bigger than its stroke, which keeps engine-wearing piston speed down. Otherwise, it was very much the direct descendant of the original M60, with aluminium alloy 90° vee cylinder block and heads, four-valves per cylinder worked by double overhead camshafts via hydraulic tappets, ferrous cylinder liners and forged sintered iron connecting rods.

Con rod big-end bearing caps were a fracture fitting, originally an American industry technique. Having notched the bearings at each end of the desired split line, they are deliberately broken along that line. The consequent shattered faces of con rod and bottom half of the bearing fitting together perfectly to provide a highly effective keying effect on the joint. This eliminates the need for a key and matching recess deliberately machined in the joint, thus providing a lower cost, yet more thorough, joint.

The V8 form was ideal for the Aero 8, since such engines are short for their size compared with a similar capacity straight six. This gave the marginal, but dynamically useful advantage of allowing the mass of the engine to be kept towards the car's rear, for a better front–rear balance, to the benefit of the car's handling. V8s are also inherently stiff and strong, helping refinement. The BMW V8 was also impressively less heavy, scaling between 448lb and 468lb in its original 3- and 4-litre versions, thanks primarily to extensive use of aluminium alloy, plus lightweight design of details like the magnesium alloy for the camshaft covers, the sintered iron con rods, plastic intake manifolding, and thin-walled stainless steel exhaust manifold. In 4.4-litre form, with a 10.0:1 compression ratio, it had a respectable specific power output, its 282bhp (James Watt) at 5,700rpm corresponding to 64bhp/litre; the 317lb ft at 3,900rpm maximum torque, equivalent to a brake mean effective pressure of 178psi, was also impressive.

It was also an advanced design in terms of engine control, its Digital Motor Electronic M3.3 engine management system being one of the most sophisticated in the business. DME M3.3's features included: advanced cylinder knock control, using not the usual single knock sensor but four, to provide individual cylinder control; individual ignition coils to each cylinder fed by a solid-state distributor; a fuel injection system capable of individual injection volume to each cylinder; and a drive-by-wire throttle control for better injection response to the driver's wishes.

Fuel–air mixture and thereby engine load were sensed by hot-film air-mass metering, which offered fast accurate response whilst being very simple with no moving parts and its principal parts integrated in a ceramic substrate. Any individual cylinder misfiring, for whatever reason, was automatically diagnosed and potential waste of fuel and exhaust emissions problems avoided by cutting out injection to the affected cylinder. These are but a few of the many details of DME M3.3's design attributes, too numerous to go through here. Suffice it to say that the M60 family of engines was comprehensively controlled in the interests of smoothness, exhaust emissions, efficiency, and performance.

Limited maximum speed

To continue Chris Lawrence's account, he added: 'For some curious reason, which I will never understand, the Mk1, the pure "me" car if you like, of which we produced 300 off, is just about as fast a car as you could buy, except we limited the top speed. BMW rather lent on me, saying: "We restrict our cars to 160, we think you should too." Charles wasn't very keen, but I just said: "Go ahead, let's do it because it's all in the management." So the big butterfly throttle starts to shut down at about 5,800rpm and it will only torque to about 6,000 or 6,100rpm, which is about 158mph odd – so it hasn't got the top end of these Ferraris and all that sort – but we did a Gumball Rally together three times, which is a bit of sheer idiocy, but it was a very good test.

'We had a pact for the first one about the bonnet. I had made the front of the car, which looked like a Plus 8, come off in one bit, so you couldn't take the body off without completely disclosing the Beemer. So we had an agreement that if anything went wrong, we'd just park it and walk away, and that was it. Because Charles was paranoid about people finding out about it. And anyway, we didn't get any trouble – we never took the front off, we never checked anything.

'At one stage on one of the Gumballs, we were on a motorway *péage* with lots of cubicles, which were all working, and about five of us all arrived in a big heap. There were Ferraris and Lamborghinis, and Porsches, and this funny-looking little Plus 8 Morgan, and we all roared in together. And it so happened that everybody paid and it was sort of like the gates of a starting horserace, they all opened at once. We all came out in a big heap and guess

Right: Rolling Series 1 chassis complete with BMW V8 engine.

who got into the single lane first? Charles – he wound the lot of them off. Thereafter we were besieged by people saying, "What the hell is that ?" "Plus 8, you know, just an old one" – of course it looked very beaten up – it was all glass fibre and looked like a Plus 8, yes. Anyway, we got away with it: we never took it to bits, never had the front off it to reveal what the engine was.'

Launched at Geneva

As everything turned out, the entirely new Morgan made its public bow at the 2000 Geneva Motor Show. It caused a sensation, understandably, for a variety of strong reasons. The replacement of the very long established top-hat channel section steel chassis of all four-wheeled Morgans up until then, with a truly sophisticated

Morgan Aero 8 and its rivals in 2001

Make and Model	Top speed	0–60mph	0–100mph	Standing ¼-mile	Fuel consumption	Price inc tax
Alfa Romeo 3.0 Spider	145mph	6.6sec	16.0sec	15.1sec	28mpg	£26,340
BMW Z3 M Roadster	157mph	4.8sec	10.9sec	13.7sec	25mpg	£36,000
Caterham Super 7 R500	145mph	3.4sec	8.1sec	11.9sec	23mpg	£34,200
Honda S800	147mph	5.6sec	14.3sec	–	27mpg	£25,995
Jaguar XKR convertible	155mph	5.1sec	12.4sec	14.0sec	19mpg	£63,350
Lotus Elise 1.8	124mph	5.8sec	17.6sec	14.6sec	31mpg	£22,980
Mercedes-Benz SLK 320	149mph	7.0sec	18.6sec	15.5sec	29mpg	£31,240
Mercedes-Benz 500SL	155mph	5.8sec	13.5sec	14.4sec	21mpg	£65,430
Morgan Aero 8	151mph	4.8sec	11.7sec	13.5sec	21mpg	£55,500
Morgan Plus 8 4.0	121mph	6.1sec	18.4sec	15.1sec	23mpg	£33,487
Porsche 911 cabriolet	177mph	4.6sec	10.1sec	12.9sec	22mpg	£62,000
Porsche Boxster S	161mph	6.0sec	14.2sec	14.3sec	26mpg	£38,330
TVR Tuscan Speed Six	180mph*	4.2sec	9.5sec	–	20mpg	£48,390

* Estimated

Far left: The Aero 8 as first shown at Geneva in 2000.

Left: Cockpit of the original Aero 8 as shown at Geneva with engine-turned instrument panel. The facia was changed for production models.

Far left: The original Aero 8 with its weather protection in place.

Left: As exhibited at the Geneva Motor Show in 2000.

Right: The aluminium chassis with ash frame for the body.

Far right: The original headlamp design was somewhat contentious.

modern aluminium-alloy sheet and extrusion chassis with a respectable beam and torsional stiffness, was one reason for astonishment.

Another was the death, at any rate on this Morgan, after nearly a century of the Morgan sliding-pillar independent front suspension and the semi-elliptic-sprung leaf spring back end, on lever-arm dampers, in favour of an unequal length wishbone geometry, coil spring, telescopic damper, all-independent set-up. The only somewhat contentious change was part of the styling of the body in the area of the headlamps, which to some eyes looked somewhat cross-eyed.Finally, there was the power unit – another V8, yes, but not from an American-Anglo background as in the case of the GM-Rover engine of the Plus 8, but instead from the world famous and highly respected Bavarian carmaker BMW, whose four-valve-per-cylinder 4.4-litre was normally found at that time in the 540i and 740i BMW saloon cars.

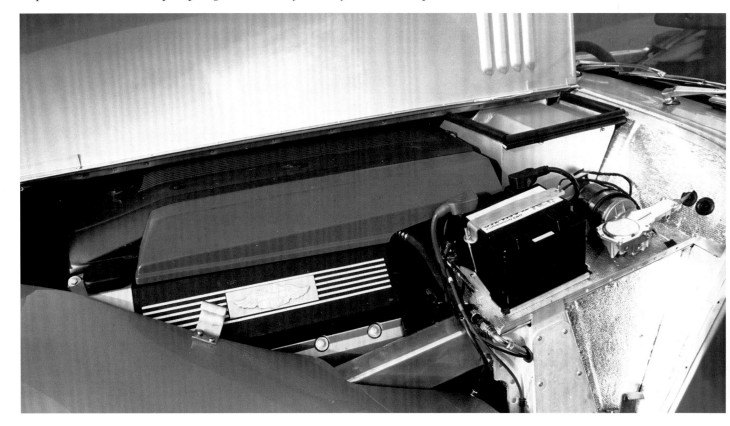

Right: The Series 1's BMW 4.4-litre V8 engine carries a Morgan badge.

Above: Aero 8 Series
1 seen against an
academic background.

Left: Series 1 Aero 8 in
three-quarter rear view.

Left: Side view of Aero 8 cockpit showing its seats, which afford good side support.

Above: Dashboard of Series 1 model in export left-hand-drive form with different steering wheel.

Opposite: Aero 8 not quite losing it on a wet corner.

Below: Driver's view of Aero 8 facia and controls.

The later versions

Aero 8 has, in fact, gone through three more versions since the Geneva 2000 launch of the Series 1. The Series 2, announced in 2004, saw considerable changes to the car, the most notable of which were the bodywork being widened, the installation of an airbag in the cockpit, and an anti-lock braking system. This was the model which got American Federal approvals (for passive safety and so on) for the Aero 8, so that Morgan could start sending cars to the US.

Series 3, the most short lived of the Aero 8 models, launched in 2005, was notable for the redesign/restyling of the front of the car. This corrected the headlamp position and also included a new aerodynamic spoiler, or splitter, round the nose. This largely came about thanks to the tooling investment that Morgan carried

Right: Airbag-equipped Series 3 with white-faced instrument dials.

Below: Cockpit of 2007 Series 3. Passenger airbag is incorporated in engine-turned dashboard.

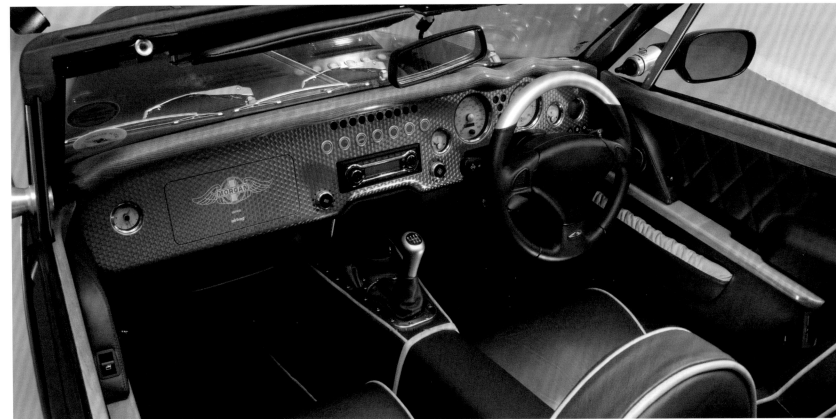

Above: Three-quarter rear view of this particular example may perhaps suggest to some eyes that the two-tone colour scheme makes the back appear a little heavier than it actually is.

Far left: BMW 4.4-litre V8 engine in position under the Series 3's bonnet.

Left: Repositioned headlamp of the Series 3.

Far left: Twin tailpipes emerge from suggestion of an aerodynamic venturi underside to tail.

Left: Wide-angle close-up of Series 3 wheel and wing

Above: The AeroMax coupé had a completely new body but was based on the Series 4 Aero 8.

Right: Detail of nose of Series 3 Aero 8, and how it retains the grille shape familiar from the Plus 8.

Far right: Superform aluminium alloy construction.

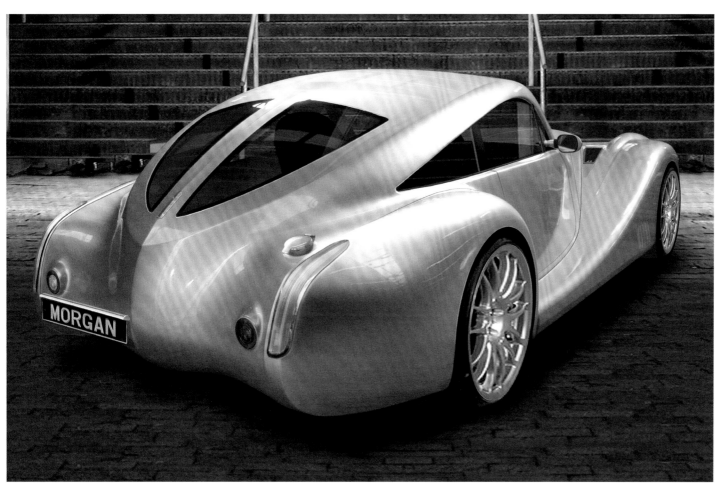

Left: Distinctive rear styling of the limited edition AeroMax.

Below: The Series 4 Aero 8 announced in 2007.

out for the AeroMax – the fixed-head coupé with what is basically a Series 4 chassis and headlamp position and a completely new coupé body. This model, of which the company is producing 100, is marked out by being the world's first Superformed car and is, of course, a derivative of the Aero 8. Superform is a process of hot forming of aluminium alloy that has been used for the wings on the traditional car. It is done for Morgan by Superform Aluminium, a company based in Worcester.

Series 4, the still current model, came in 2007 and has the benefit of a larger and more powerful BMW engine, 4.8 instead of 4.4 litres, producing 362bhp at 6,200rpm against the 286bhp of the Series 1 and 325bhp of the Series 2 and Series 3 models. The new model was distinguished by revised instrumentation, a repositioned fuel tank giving greater luggage space, and larger air intakes and vents in the wings.

Right: The Series 4 is powered by BMW's 4.8-litre V8 and is claimed to accelerate from rest to 60mph in just 4.2sec.

Below: Larger vents in the wings and wheelarch reflectors distinguished the Series 4 Aero 8. This car has the extra cost side-exit exhaust system.

Claimed maximum speed was 170mph with the 0–60mph sprint taking just 4.2sec. By the end of 2007 over 600 Aero 8s had left the factory.

New for the Series 4 model in 2008 was an automatic gearbox option using ZF's 6HP26 six-speed gearbox, which offered a choice of fully automatic or sport manual modes. This was the first production Morgan to be offered with an automatic transmission.

The LIFECar project

On a totally different front, something came out of Morgan in 2007 that – if the Aero 8's modern chassis and suspension had not already convinced the company's critics that it was fully prepared for the latest in automotive technology – will serve to demonstrate that the Malvern firm has its eye very much on the future of the car. The announcement, which made spectacular headlines in the spring of 2007, was the Morgan LIFECar

Above: : The Morgan LIFECar opened to show the fuel cell technology.

Left: LIFECar has been engineered to give a top speed of about 80mph and a 250-mile range.

Above: Aero 8 chassis in the Morgan assembly shop.

Top right: Morgan's stand at the 2008 British Motor Show at Excel, London. Behind the Aero 8 is the Roadster V6 with the LIFECar in the background.

What the Aero 8 cost in 2008

	Basic	Tax	Total in UK
Aero 8 4.8 litre	£57,832.34	£10,127.66	£68,000.00
Extras			
Automatic gearbox	£2,295.00	£401.62	£2,696.62
Metallic paint	£440.00	£77.00	£517.00
Two-tone paint	£995.00	£104.12	£699.13
Hardtop (body colour)	£2,500.00	£437.50	£2,937.50
Bonnet louvres	£200.00	£35.00	£235.00
Graphite alloy wheels	£425.00	£74.38	£499.38
Side exhaust wing preparation	£250.00	£43.75	£293.75
Side exit exhaust (some markets)	£1,000.00	£175.00	£1,175.00
Schedoni fitted luggage	£846.81	£148.19	£995.00
Blaupunkt RDS radio/CD player	£320.00	£56.00	£376.00
Graphite dashboard	£295.00	£51.63	£346.63
Door pockets	£250.00	£43.75	£293.75
Leather covered steering wheel top, gear knob, steering wheel cowl	£425.00	£74.38	£499.38
Contrasting seat piping	£220.00	£38.50	£258.50
Photographic build record	£125.00	£21.88	£146.88

project. Morgan LIFECar – the capitals stand for Lightweight Fuel Efficient Car, an understatement of its nature – is a project to build a hydrogen-fuelled fuel-cell sports car 'to demonstrate a new step in vehicle architecture is enabled in a lightweight vehicle by the use of a fuel cell in a lightweight vehicle,' and 'that a zero emission vehicle can also be fun to drive.'

The project is a joint venture with distinguished participants: BOC (hydrogen supply and refuelling equipment), Cranfield University (systems simulation, on-board computing, and control of the powertrain), Oxford University (design and control of the electric motors), Oscar Automotive (overall system design and architecture), QinetiQ (development of fuel cell), Linde AG (industrial hydrogen supply), and the Morgan Motor Company (providing the car itself and assembly of the concept). The resulting coupé appeared at the March 2008 Geneva Show and featured again on Morgan's stand at the London Motor Show at Excel in July.

Morgan today

It is perhaps appropriate to end with a brief update on the happy state of the still healthily flourishing company as this book went to press in 2008. Production was then running at around 15 cars per week: three Aero 8/AeroMax models, four to five V6 Roadsters (the surviving model in the Plus 8 range), and the rest made up by manufacture of the four-cylinder models. Customers ordering a new Morgan had then to wait around 12 months for all models.

THE BURSTON GROUP

Specificati

ENGINE

Description
Overhead valve
block and cast
cross-flow cyli
camshafts per
per cylinder v
variable intal
pistons, forge
rods, fractur
Five-bearing
catalytic cor

Capacity
4,398cc (26

Bore and s
92.0mm x

Compress
10.0:1

Maximu
282bhp (

Maximu
317lb ft

Fuellin
Bosch f
manag

TRAN

Gearl
Getra

Rati
1st
2nd
3rd
4th   1.220:
5th   1.000:1
Top   0.828:1
Reverse   3.750:1

dry plate

bearings

BTR limited slip

sc, 13.0in (330mm)

sc, 12.0in (306mm)

lic, anti-lock system

e linkage to rear drums

ever upper arm, lower
oil springs, Koni telescopic

ble wishbones, Eibach coil
copic dampers

pinion with variable power

s lock to lock

Steering wheel
Three-spoke, 14in diameter

WHEELS AND TYRES
9J x 18in magnesium alloy wheels

Tyres
225/40ZR-18in Dunlop SP Sport 9000 run-flat radial ply

PERFORMANCE
Autocar Road Test, 24 October 2001

Top speed

151mph (243kph)	
0–50mph (80kph)	3.7sec
0–60mph (96kph)	4.8sec
0–70mph (112kph)	6.2sec
0–80mph (128kph)	7.4sec
0–90mph (144kph)	9.1sec
0–100mph (160kph)	11.7sec
Standing quarter mile (402m)	13.5sec

Overall fuel consumption
19.4mpg (14.6l/100km)

DIMENSIONS

Length
13ft 6.2in (4,120mm)

Width
5ft 9.7in (1,770mm)

Height (hood up)
3ft 11.2in (1,200mm)

Wheelbase
8ft 3.6in (2,530mm)

Track
Front: 4ft 11.4in (1,510mm)
Rear: 4ft 10.3in (1,480mm)

Ground clearance
5.9in (150mm)

Weight
2,502lb (1,135kg)

AERO 8
THE COMPETITION
STORY

Origins of the GTN racer

As we have seen in earlier chapters, Aero 8's immediate predecessor, the Plus 8, attracted club motoring racing enthusiasts with its generous power-to-weight ratio and character. Aero 8, with a modern, lighter and very much torsionally stiffer chassis, classic all-independent suspension, disc brakes at every corner, and an excellent power-to-weight ratio, was even more likely to interest those keen on racing.

Chris Lawrence, Morgan's chief development engineer, had fully appreciated the new car's competition potential from early on in its conception. From 1997 in a dark, disused shed behind the Morgan factory with two assistants, Lawrence set about evolving and producing his next contribution to the Morgan stable, the Aero 8 GTN competition car. Its name signified complicity with the FIA's GTN regulations whilst also meeting the demands of the French Automobile Club de l'Ouest (the ACO), the organisers of Le Mans and its historically famous 24-hour race. Chris, of course, was the man who 35 years earlier had driven a 2-litre Morgan Plus 4 to a class victory at the 1962 Le Mans, so nursing great ambitions for his project – that could provide a fitting climax to his car engineering career – was entirely understandable.

The 2002 Le Mans race

Chris's competition version of the Aero 8 first appeared in public at the January 2002 *Autosport* International Exhibition at the National Exhibition Centre, Birmingham. On the first day of the show, a serious buyer appeared on the Morgan stand and engaged Chris Lawrence in conversation. Thus its first club racing driver buyer of note was Richard Stanton, who had been a TVR devotee but now went for the Aero 8 GTN, and his talk with Chris was on just one subject – Le Mans. Chris Lawrence seized the opportunity to convince Richard that the car could meet Le Mans requirements and that the ACO would welcome such an entry. Stanton paid a deposit and the first car was his.

Its first circuit appearance was a media event at which the newly proposed Le Mans 2002 co-operation between the DeWalt/Stanton team and the Morgan Motor Co was announced publicly. DeWalt was a tool company with whom Richard Stanton had close connections, so the car appeared at the Rockingham circuit in the yellow and black livery of its sponsors, in the presence of two drivers, Richard Stanton and Steve Hyde. That Rockingham day was not an auspicious one for the new Morgan, whose engine tuned by the Swiss engine firm Mader refused to start – seriously enough for more than one battery to be run down in the efforts to get it going. It did finally fire up and was given a couple of laps for the benefit of press photographers and TV cameramen.

Having secured acceptance of their entry to the Le Mans race, the next hurdle was the pre-race test weekend at the 8.45-mile Sarthe circuit, in which each driver (there were now three: Stanton, Hyde, and Richard Hay) had to cover a minimum of ten laps in the car, which duly happened,

Left: The Aero 8 GTN's debut at the Autosport International Exhibition in Birmingham in January 2002.

Below left: This adjustable rear wing was a striking feature of the Aero 8 GTN.

Below: The Aero 8 GTN was also shown at the British International Motor Show at Birmingham in 2002.

Above: Charles Morgan with the Aero 8 racer sponsored by DeWalt tools.

Above right: The DeWalt-sponsored Aero 8's first outing was at the Rockingham circuit.

Right: Pre-qualifying for the 2002 Le Mans race.

albeit not very fast, the car running at the back of the GT class field.

The Mader BMW engine had also not distinguished itself in reliability, so some further testing at the BMW-run test track at Miramas in the south of France in the week before the Le Mans race week was agreed and duly happened. The race week began with scrutineering, in which after two tense hours of inspection by the scrutineers, the team was set a number of tasks to perform on the car if it was to run in the qualifying laps before the event proper. Frantic work in uncomfortably hot June weather immediately following scrutineering lasted until 1am and resumed on the next day at 6.30am. In the end it was successful, the car finally acquiring its scrutineering pass certificate.

Qualifying running began late that afternoon, the drivers lapping into the night, striving to get the Aero 8 down to its required lap time. This proved to be a struggle at first but eventually Richard Hay did the job with a 4min 16sec lap time just as darkness was threatening, so the team was in for the 24 hours. This all happened on the Thursday before the weekend, leaving Friday for a precautionary engine change, which was duly carried out, ready for the 4pm start on the Saturday.

It's not really something that is vital to the story of the Aero 8 but, besides entering such a non-sports-racing car contender in the race, the Morgan team was responsible for one small first in Le Mans history – the introduction of a web camera into the pit, for the benefit of all the countless Morgan fans worldwide who would not be able to attend the race. It depended, of course, on fixing up the Morgan pit with an ADSL line, which was delayed enough not to be working until the Saturday morning.

Then 4pm came at last and the cars were off, only for the Morgan to come in at the end of the first lap with a rear-end vibration that required a complete change of the whole rear end of the car, a near-30 minute job even in the very capable hands of the Morgan/DeWalt mechanics. However, in contrast to lesser events, a 30-minute stop (although a loss which is not healthy for any

Left: Race preparation in the team garage at Le Mans in 2002.

Below: The Aero 8 and its team at Le Mans in 2002 with veteran 1962 Le Mans racer TOK 258.

Above: The racing lines of the Aero 8 are shown in the action shot at the Sarthe circuit in 2002.

Right: Cornering hard in the 2002 Le Mans race.

contender's position) is not the end of the race at Le Mans. So the Morgan was off again in due course, circulating at or around the planned 4min 27sec per lap target.

All was going fine for the next several hours, until at around 2am on the Sunday morning, Richard Stanton again reported rear-end vibration. This time the change of parts was accomplished in an astonishing 14 minutes. Off the Aero 8 went again into the fray. First light came and then the real beginnings of the morning. At around 9am it was clear that something was seriously amiss with car 73, which was limping along, clearly hoping to make it back to the pits. There was a serious engine problem but Richard Stanton and the Aero 8 made it. In no time, the car was on jacks, the bonnet off, and the Mader engine men in attendance working with their Morgan colleagues on the smoking engine. It was dead; the race was over for the Aero 8, after 17 hours of the 24 had been run.

Capitalising on Le Mans

Although both the DeWalt and Morgan teams saw the failure to finish as just that, a failure, in public relations terms for Morgan, it was anything but a failure. This, plus the enthusiasm of both the Morgan people who had been involved and the team's sponsors, added up to a general view that the 2002 Le Mans effort counted as unfinished business, which ought to be pursued again in 2003.

Chris Lawrence produced a set of notes on what had gone wrong and how those mistakes might be put right. David Dowse (now Morgan's PR manager, having started with the company in May 2000, not long after the Aero 8's Geneva Show launch as PR consultant) pointed out to Charles Morgan the success of Morgan's exposure on a corporate level, proved by the very large coverage by TV, radio, and the press stimulated by the Le Mans effort, and that this was a valuable achievement.

Nevertheless, Morgan's family shareholders were resistant to the notion of racing. The company's chairman, the ageing Peter Morgan, recalled all too well how expensive motor racing was for a company the size of his. There was all too obviously a lot to do to improve on 2002's result. For this reason, discussion centred on the possibilities of sponsors and in particular what Richard Stanton and his sponsors might be interested in doing. In due course, Stanton pointed out that there was a good possibility that DeWalt might sponsor the notional 2003 effort, asking Chris Lawrence if he could produce a specification for a new contender.

However, there were doubts within the Morgan camp about how certain Stanton's involvement backed by DeWalt might be; he had after all been a long-term TVR driver and had only come to the Aero 8 in 2002 because TVR did not

Below: A night-time pit-stop for the Aero 8 in the 2002 Le Mans 24-hour race.

Right: The DeWalt-sponsored Aero 8 driven by Richard Stanton and Steve Hyde in action at Brands Hatch in 2002.

Below: The Stanton/ Hyde car in the Donington round of the British GT Championship in 2002.

have a Le Mans contender. It was true that if Stanton did come to Morgan again, DeWalt would back him but could he be counted on?

David Dowse, in a written proposal, suggested to Charles Morgan that a 2003 Le Mans Morgan should be done as a proper works team entry to the famous event, pointing out how the publicity success of 2002 even when the car had not finished confirmed that it should be possible to get decent sponsorship for the 2003 event and that he, Dowse, would be happy to take on the responsibility of team manager. No written reply came but when David met Charles in the factory shortly afterwards, Charles simply said: 'We are going to need some sponsorship,' acting as if the idea was taken for granted.

This was very much easier said than done, which posed a major problem for the company, which simply could not afford the great cost of motor racing if unassisted by sponsorship. The search went on; meanwhile some money was raised, by the sale of some old racing kit, to allow the project to continue.

Left: The Carlube-sponsored racer campaigned by Keith Ahlers/Rob Wells in the 2003 British GT Championship.

Cup Class racing

In the midst of all this Chris Lawrence was involved in a new project to evolve and build a development of the roadgoing Aero 8 for 'Cup Class' national racing; his effort was quickly rewarded by orders for two examples from an American customer.

Chris Lawrence's Cup model Aero 8 project was proceeding and theoretically had competitive performance. An unexpected combination of boost and distraction arose when it was realised that Keith Ahlers, a well-known Morgan fan and customer, had ordered one of Chris Lawrence's Cup Class Aero 8s, which he was planning to run in the British GT championship. As the first race in this series at Donington was getting close, Chris Lawrence was approached by a successful Morgan dealer, Richard Thorne, who wanted to do the same as Keith Ahlers. Morgan having had no previous entry in the national championship, the idea that two Aero 8s might be seen racing at the same event was very attractive.

In spite of several obstacles, the car was built just in time, being wheeled out and delivered to the circuit early on race morning. It was to be driven by two drivers, Keith Robinson and an enterprising Australian, Neil Cunningham, who took the car out first in practice. He reappeared at the end of his first lap, still running hard and fast, but now minus the hardtop roof, returning to the pits with an apology, though it wasn't his fault that the roof had apparently not been secured properly. A search party recovered the hardtop but it was too badly damaged to be refitted and there was no replacement available, so permission was sought successfully to run the car open in the race.

Regardless of the extra aerodynamic drag, Cunningham and Robinson drove the car fast enough to be on the tail of the Porsche GT3 that was to win the class, the Aero 8 ending up seventh overall and second in its class, ahead of the third place in the class taken by

its Morgan rival, the Keith Ahlers/Rob Wells Aero 8. This was a first for Morgan's Aero 8, in securing podium honours in a British national event. The results cheered everyone concerned greatly, particularly in the case of the Cunningham/Robinson Richard Thorne car, which had, as the saying goes, done its very impressive bit 'straight out of the box'.

Below: The Aero 8 raced by Morgan dealer Richard Thorne with drivers Keith Robinson and Neil Cunningham. Here the car is racing at Donington without its hardtop, which came adrift during practice.

Homologation problems

However, the undeniable morale boost of the Donington success was quickly destroyed by a fax from the ACO, the organisers behind the Le Mans race, saying that Morgan had been unsuccessful in its application for entry to the 2003 24-hour race. This considerable blow was only a little mitigated by the approach in August of the Spa 24-hour race and the preceding other event in the FIA calendar, the Donington 1,000km race. A lot of effort now went in to converting the car that had been built to comply with the ACO Le Mans requirements for the very different demands of the FIA; could this be done in the time available? The men involved in modifying the car were at it night and day from now on, weekends included.

The effort to ready the car for the Donington 1,000km race continued. Main physical effort was in the workshop, preparing the car, but on the office side, there was plenty of action too. The FIA homologation papers had confirmed the Aero 8's eligibility but there were some difficulties still to be overcome. The biggest of these was the carbon-fibre hardtop developed for the car for the FIA's GTN class. This, theoretically, had to be a standard item offered for sale with the car. In fact such a roof was developed by the racing shop and put into small-scale production as an extra for production Aero 8s. It was finally agreed that a production car fitted with the hard top would have to be taken to the race for the FIA to inspect. A fax from the FIA's Geneva headquarters agreed that subject to sight of the production car and hardtop at the Donington race, homologation of the car was approved.

The week preceding the 1,000 km race arrived with the car still being worked on, so that in the end, it did not arrive at the circuit until a few hours before the official scrutineering inspection on the Thursday morning. Paperwork was assembled and, after a final two hours of cleaning and polishing the car, it was wheeled along to scrutineering. Not particularly friendly FIA officials demanded to see the paperwork as well as inspect the car and seemed clearly determined to find fault. The impression proved all too correct, as one official and a colleague studied the papers, only to say to David Dowse that the car was not homologated.

A copy of the fax was handed to them with the key phrase that subject to viewing of the production hardtop, the car will be homologated to race in the event. The officials examined this, then said that they had not received any confirmation of this statement themselves and therefore the car was not homologated. It was pointed out politely that perhaps they could contact Geneva to obtain the confirmation, only for this to be met with the answer from a phone call to Geneva to say that the man who had sent it was now on holiday and unobtainable. Thus it was that the car never made it to the actual race at Donington – a second massive frustration after the Le Mans problem.

This maddening situation was made even more frustrating when after the race weekend, the return from his trip of the Geneva official who had sent that fax confirmed so readily and easily that the car was homologated to take part in that race – too late of course.

Disaster at Spa

Happily, however, Morgan's management confirmed that the effort to enter the next FIA race, the Spa 24 hours, must continue. However, that still meant that this depended on sponsorship, as the fateful Donington failure had cost a great deal and Spa would cost a lot more.

Neil Cunningham was a very willing helper to the cause, continually pressing whoever he could for support, producing various forms of minor assistance; one

The Le Mans 2003 entry

After the bad news about the Le Mans application, the battle to find out why the ACO had rejected Morgan and how its objections, whatever they were, could possibly be overcome was being waged by every means possible. Le Mans was after all the most valuable event for Morgan in the sports-car racing year, much more so than anything else, so the drive to try for an explanation and a way round whatever was the reason for the rejection was conducted over a wide front.

A press release issued by Morgan explaining the blow drew tremendous support from both British and European and American Morgan fans, so much so that David Dowse was worried that a bombardment of the ACO with offensive messages from Morgan's supporters might occur that he felt constrained to suggest to anyone who offered, to write as tactfully as possible to the ACO as he felt that rudeness would not help the Morgan cause to this vital event. In fact, both press and several hundred fans who wrote got that message and were very supportive but sensitive in their approach.

Back at Malvern, Chris Lawrence, plagued by illness, led the efforts to get to understand the ACO's problem with Morgan; he was well qualified, of course, to try to talk to them, given his now ancient success at Le Mans. He eventually got through to a senior official and established that there was what turned out to be a minor expenses invoice for an ACO technical visit to Morgan in 2002 which it said had not been paid.

A search by the Morgan accounts office showed that such an invoice did not appear to have been received and certainly there had been no subsequent statements or reminders from Le Mans. This raised suspicions that the firm had been tried and sentenced for a crime it had not known it had committed, and further that someone in Le Mans had it in for the British firm. Desperate phone calls to ask for a second chance were met apologetically, but adamantly, with the answer that no second chance was possible.

example came from an introduction to Colin North of Teng Tools, which offered a most generous donation from Mr North of all the tools needed by the team which it had never had – for which Morgan was most grateful.

However, what made the crucial difference was when Charles Morgan, in his efforts to rescue the situation, persuaded a wealthy Swiss banker to visit the Morgan factory. Prince Eric Sturzda happened also to be a great Morgan enthusiast and a close friend of the well-known French Formula 1 driver, Jacques Lafitte. Both men came and, over lunch in a local pub, a deal was struck with them to combine sponsorship from Banque Barings Bros in Switzerland with Jacques Lafitte as a team driver at Spa. This was a hugely valuable morale booster.

Next happening for the car intended for Spa was a testing session at BMW's facilities at Miramas in the south of France not long before the race. It was then decided

to precede this visit with a test on a 'four-poster' suspension rig in Norfolk to check the car's suspension and chassis. This was duly carried out and a report issued suggested some small alterations designed to improve the car dynamically. Then the Aero 8 was driven to Miramas for a further two days of circuit testing. This ended in a successful session, after which the Morgan was trailered up to Spa. This time, the paperwork was accepted, the only hurdle now being the physical scrutineering that, with relatively little remedial work being required, the car passed.

All went fine at first, Jacques Lafitte taking the first session very convincingly before handing over to Neil Cunningham for the dusk stint. By this time, Spa's notorious tendency to serious rain had brought a torrential downpour, making driving obviously very risky. Neil did an excellent job keeping the car on the track, until his mount suffered a repeat of the engine cutting out just as he had passed a

fellow competitor in a Porsche. The Porsche had been close on the Morgan's tail when the cutting out occurred and, in the very poor visibility caused by the weather, struck the Aero 8 from behind. This put it into a series of spins ending in impacts with walls, which destroyed the back end of the car and its running in the event, luckily without any serious injury for Neil other than shaking him up considerably.

It looked like curtains for the entire project – a seriously broken car, what sponsorship there had been gone, the team dispersing in various directions – when Ben Coles, a freelance fabricator and first-class welder, looked over the wrecked Aero 8 and announced that he reckoned he could repair it. It was now September 2003 and to sustain things for an attempt to enter the following year's Le Mans, it was essential to precede this with some competition success. One obvious opportunity was the 1,000km race on the Bugatti Circuit at Le Mans in November.

Below: The Aero 8 in the Spa 24-hour race where sponsorship by Banque Barings Bros in Switzerland brought with it Jacques Lafitte as driver, partnered by Neil Cunningham.

Right: The Richard Thorne Motorsport Aero 8, driven by Neil Cunningham and Adam Sharpe, in action at Brands Hatch in the final round of the 2003 British GT Championship.

Below: Winner of the British GT Cup Class at Brands Hatch in 2003 was the Richard Thorne car, sponsored by Teng Tools.

The British GT championship

Prior to the 1,000km Le Mans event, Neil Cunningham did the honours in the British GT championship event at Knockhill in Scotland. Driving Richard Thorne's Aero 8 Cup car, he finally beat the Porsche on whose tail he had been too often previously. Earlier in the season when driving that car, he had shared the driving with a young driver called Adam Sharpe, whose father Robert had helped with the costs of taking part. At the final round of the British GT Championship at Brands Hatch two weeks after Knockhill, the Thorne Aero 8 Cup car was again driven by Neil with Adam Sharpe. Robert Sharpe was there to watch his son, for whom he was very ambitious.

Sorties abroad

In conversation with David Dowse during British GT Championship at Brands Hatch, Robert Sharpe said that if there was any chance of Adam being involved in a Le Mans drive in the works Morgan, he would pay for his son to take part with Neil in the Bugatti Circuit event and was prepared to help finance the project.

Chris Lawrence was most excited by this, immediately saying he would send off the entry fees from his own income immediately – an immense and valued gesture. This was done in spite of being in the throes of chemotherapy treatment of a cancer, which mercifully was successful, even if it left poor Chris feeling well below par for some time. The Morgan management was happy to allow free use of the car and workshop but not to finance the project at all.

Far left: Neil Cunningham and Adam Sharpe were the drivers for the 1,000km race on the Bugatti Circuit at Le Mans. The car finished eighth.

Below: The Aero 8 went to Australia for the 2003 Bathurst 24-hour race but suffered mechanical failure.

The trip to take part in the 1,000km race proved well worth it. There were some pre-race concerns, most seriously the realisation that racing licences for Neil Cunningham and for Adam Sharpe were not valid for this race, since they were not international C grade. Fortunately this was sorted out just in time. The other concerned the car, which passed scrutineering in all respects until a tape-measure-wielding official discovered that the wheels were 1in over the maximum size permitted; that situation was solved by David Dowse's brother-in-law, Tim, who gallantly came to the rescue by agreeing to drive through the night to deliver the appropriate smaller wheels.

After all this effort, the car ran faultlessly and finished eighth out of a strong field of 18 runners in the GT class – an excellent result, which was just what the team needed. The next challenge on the immediate horizon was the 12-hour race at Sebring in Florida, another essential step on the road towards the 2004 Le Mans event. However, then Robert Sharpe introduced a distraction, in the form of entering the 24-hour race at Bathurst in Australia, with Richard Thorne and Richard's Morgan GT Cup car. Drivers were Neil Cunningham, Adam Sharpe, Keith Ahlers, and a newcomer to the Thorne team, Tom Shrimpton. As Morgan was only too aware, the GT Cup cars were built for what was in effect sprint racing, not long-distance 24-hour endurance, but those involved would not listen. The outcome was as the critics had warned, the engine threw a connecting rod explosively after only six hours.

There was to be no nonsense about the choice of car for the 12-hour Sebring event – the usual Le-Mans-contending Aero 8 GTN was the mount for its three drivers, Keith Ahlers, Neil Cunningham, and Adam Sharpe. The team's comfort, well-being and race equipment were saved by two American Morgan enthusiasts, Jack Payne and Tom Holfelder. Jack Payne organised food and snacks, while Tom Holfelder, a California-based Cup Class Aero 8 racer, lent essential tools and pit equipment without charge. Scrutineers were not so friendly, the team ending up with a lot of work. However, they were in safely and finished tenth overall out of a field of 22 runners.

Below: GTN racing version of Aero 8 at Sebring 12-hour race in 2003. Driven by Keith Ahlers, Neil Cunningham, and Adam Sharpe, the car finished tenth overall.

Le Mans testing 2004

Finally, there was the 2004 Le Mans at last, the culmination of the team's ambitions. The pre-race test session started well, the three drivers each being required to complete ten laps to qualify. Neil Cunningham started by recording a highly satisfactory 4min 27sec lap, followed by the team's youngest member (and incidentally youngest driver in the event that year), 19-year-old Adam Sharpe, who managed 4min 35sec. However, before he had completed the required qualifying minimum of ten laps, he came in reporting something amiss with the steering, which turned out to be a blown rack oil seal. The team already knew that it

was required to change the differential, so the session was ended in order to deal with both the rack seal and differential during the lunch stop.

The job went well, so that after lunch, Adam was able to complete his qualifying laps before handing over to Keith Ahlers. However, Keith was out of luck, the car stopping near Mulsanne with what turned out to be a broken driveshaft when he'd completed no more than four laps. This was dealt with rapidly and Keith went out again, only to suffer a serious crash going into the Porsche curves. The damage was repaired, albeit without replacing the rear spoiler

removed by the tow truck, and out went Mr Ahlers again.

Two laps later, a broken front wishbone, an unseen consequence of the crash, intervened. Keith needed just two more laps to qualify and the Morgan team pulled out all the stops to weld-repair the wishbone, only to be prevented by an interfering safety official requiring further work. Keith ended up running again with too little time left, so that he did not make the one final lap in the time remaining. This ended his potential Le Mans drive that time – a huge pity. His place was eventually filled by an already qualified driver, Steve Hyde, an old friend of the team.

Below: The Aero 8 crewed by Neil Cunningham, Adam Sharpe, and Steve Hyde competing in the 2004 Le Mans 24-hour race.

Above: At the last scheduled stop in the 2004 Le Mans race the Aero 8 was backed into the pit garage for safety.

Right: A routine tyre change for the Morgan Aero 8 GTN in the 2004 Le Mans race. The pit crew was given an award for exemplary work during the race.

The 2004 Le Mans race

Come the race week, more than a month after the tests, the team had the initial joy of passing scrutineering completely. After an initially poor showing, led by Neil Cunningham at 4min 24sec, he, Adam Sharpe (4min 26sec) and Steve Hyde (4min 28sec) all qualified successfully. Everything continued as it should in the first six hours of the Saturday afternoon and evening of the race, Neil Cunningham repeatedly lapping at 4min 23sec – then what at the time seemed disaster struck. The car stopped on the far side of the circuit, having apparently run out of fuel at least two laps too soon. This was close to 10pm. Two hours later, the car was still at rest when Neil somehow got it moving again, enough to return to the Morgan pit where the whole fuel pump and associated equipment were hurriedly replaced.

Then things were running as they should again and continued so throughout the summer night. Around 6.30am, a broken accelerator cable had to be replaced. The next problem surfaced three hours later, when there was a radiator failure for some unclear reason. It was replaced but there was the further worry that the engine was consuming oil at an alarming rate; at least once before in the team's experience, this had been the precursor to total engine failure. Drivers were recommended to ease their running, just in case; the object now was to finish the whole 24 hours.

At 1.30pm – with just 2½ hours to go – the replacement radiator failed, due to stone damage. Another radiator change was done, even faster than the first, and inside half an hour the car set off, carefully, to deal with the final two hours. Everyone in the Morgan team was on edge, so it was at first very alarming to get a message from the race organisers. Against the noise of the racing, it was hard at first to hear what they were saying, then it gradually became clear that they wanted the names of four team members to receive an award on the team's behalf for the best technical crew in the race. The news was a great reviver of the team's spirits, cheering everyone enormously.

The car came in repeatedly, for more oil and more water; it was hanging on by what seemed to be a whisker. The final hour was approaching, with one more scheduled stop to come. The car was still running. The stop came, with the bonnet wreathed in smoke and steam. The now usual routine of replacing oil and coolant was executed with great skill and neatness. For safety, the car was put on a trolley and backed out of the pit lane into the pit itself. To minimise manoeuvring, the car was then trolley'd out of the pit again and put facing the right way before it was permitted to leave. The Aero 8 left to cheers, not just from the garages of fellow competitors but also from the grandstands opposite.

Now, with just an hour to go, the race organisers arrived complete with huge shining trophies for the four leading mechanics (Dave Bradley, Mark Baldwin, Rogier Vancamelbecke, and John Burbidge),

who were representing the entire Morgan team, plus magnums of champagne. The award was announced as being for the very fine presentation of the car at scrutineering, of the pit garage, and of the team members, and also the way they had worked so superbly throughout the entire race.

However, the race was still on. Every sort of finger in the Morgan team was crossed that the lone Aero 8 would survive. It was now in the hands of Adam Sharpe, who was driving well yet still carefully. It was still running at the start of the last lap and, contrary to instructions, every member of every team was now either on the pit wall or on top of the pits. The leading cars roared through to huge cheers, the other runners came through to similar joy, and finally, in last position, the Aero 8 with a final burst of acceleration down the finishing straight from Adam. The reception from crowd and mechanics was tremendous, a fitting reward for the determination and sustained effort of all concerned in the Morgan team.

The reader who is an absolutist about race positions, believing that the only place that counts is first, may not agree. Nevertheless, to most observers, the fact that that single Aero 8 finished the 2004 Le Mans 24-hour race – even if the Morgan was the final finisher – was and remains a true achievement. It should not be forgotten that the Morgan was competing in the company of some vastly richer, better-equipped teams from very much larger and wealthier companies, racing with cars much nearer to pure racing cars than sports cars. Although modified for greater speed and racing handling, the Aero 8 was much nearer to the long-established ideal of a Le Mans GT sports car and thus so much closer to the spirit of Le Mans.

Even though the Aero 8 remains in production and on successful sale as this is written, and will hopefully stay that way for a good while, that 2004 Le Mans result was a glorious finale to this small history of just two of Morgan's long-established range of true British sports cars.

Below: Though the Aero 8 came in last in the 2004 Le Mans, it was a considerable achievement just to have finished after 24 hours of racing.

INDEX